Counseling Psychology
Theories and Case Studies

James B. Meyer
The University of West Florida

Joyce K. Meyer

with

Foreword and Critiques

by
George M. Gazda
University of Georgia

Allyn and Bacon, Inc.   Boston

LIBRARY OF CONGRESS CATALOGING IN PUBLICATION DATA

Meyer, James B   1942-
    Counseling psychology.

    Includes bibliographies.
    1. Counseling—Cases, clinical reports, statistics.
I. Meyer, Joyce K   1942-   joint author.
II. Gazda, George Michael, 1931-   III. Title.
[DNLM: 1. Counseling—Case studies. 2. Psychology,
Applied—Case studies.   BF637.C6 M612c]

BF637.C6M47   158   74-18477

To Our Parents, Children, and Each Other

Contents

Foreword

The authors of this text state that their basic purpose is "to pose current ethical and philosophical counseling problems for evaluations of those training in counseling psychology and guidance." The cases included are appropriate for posing issues of a philosophical concern. There are a few situations related to ethical concerns as well. The cases and the counseling philosophies included are representative of the current scene. These cases represent some of the more serious problem behaviors encountered, especially for the school counselor.

The counseling approaches employed are given added authenticity because they usually do not represent the ideal solutions or ideal counseling procedures. In this regard, the counselor-trainee has an opportunity to suggest alternative procedures. This is, in fact, what I attempt to do in my critique of each case. The critiques offer additional opportunities to the trainee to evaluate and contrast other possibilities with the actual case. In other words, the trainees have examples of one critique to guide them, while at the same time, they and their instructor can critique the critique.

My preference in teaching counseling is to place trainees in counseling situations after they have achieved basic helping skills of attending behavior, perceiving accurately, and responding facilitatively, with mastery of at least some problem intervention strategies. I also prefer to teach counseling theory concurrently with practice. In order to do this successfully and to protect the trainee as well as his counselees, a pre-practicum experience is usually essential. It is for the pre-practicum experience that I can most heartily recommend the use of this text. In some programs this experience may appear in separate competency-based modules leading to the practicum itself, and in others it may be included within the introduction to a counseling theory course.

The case study approach of this book is especially useful because it acquaints the trainee with several of the basic counseling models within the context of an authentic setting. My preference toward teaching several theoretical positions and encouraging trainees to select the one or ones that seem most appropriate to them is thus enhanced through this presentation. The summaries of the given theoretical models in each case are good but brief; therefore the instructor should be prepared to supplement these models with additional readings, lectures, demonstrations, and other materials.

The case studies included are especially good for illustrating the external factors that precipitate counselee disturbance. The trainee is thus exposed to a life-like situation that will require him to attend to other individuals and conditions in addition to the counselee himself. An especially valuable learning experience for the trainee is the importance and necessity of a cooperative interdisciplinary or team approach in the helping endeavor.

In conclusion, the use of the case studies and the Focus Questions and Discussion following each case allows the trainee to gain at least a vicarious understanding of a variety of counseling procedures. This approximation to the real thing prepares the trainee to enter the actual counseling relationship with more security through his increased knowledge of appropriate counseling procedures.

George M. Gazda

Preface

This short collection of cases bridges the gap between theoretical solutions and the real world where solutions must take place. Used as a supplement to guidance books and to surveys in introductory counseling, it allows the reader to experience specific situations and settings where various theoretical techniques can be applied. Each case is presented with a particular theoretical style and application. It is then critiqued and the reader is invited to critique it himself, applying constructions from theories other than the ones presented in the case. It is hoped this book will help bring counseling concepts alive by focusing on current problems facing young people today—rapidly changing social values, sexual misadventure, and feelings of nonworth.

Another basic purpose of this book is to pose current ethical and philosophical counseling problems for evaluation by those training in counseling psychology and guidance. It is directed toward making use of the case study technique to understand the individual child or young adult well enough to help him progress toward personal goals. The case studies demonstrate that behavior is open to a multitude of influences, each of which shapes and defines the thoughts and subsequent behavior of the client. The reader is offered capsulized glimpses into the lives of confused and troubled people groping to make sense out of lives filled with guilt, confusion, and despair. The personal problems of these clients challenge the reader to devise different techniques and methodologies that will help clients find a sense of meaning and worth in their personal lives.

Readers are offered examples of human behavior they are likely to encounter as they learn about the nature of behavioral change. The book is useful in training programs for counselors, school psychologists, counseling psychologists, social workers, and others interested in human behavior. It can also be used as supplemental reading for counselor education courses or for practicum and internship.

Cases were selected for inclusion on the basis of the nature of the counseling task before the counselor and client. Problems in educational and personal counseling have been included in order to present a variety of challenging experiences to the reader. Some cases were included because of the variety of counseling techniques which were or were not used; others were chosen to involve the reader on philosophical and emotional levels. Cases were selected to highlight specific problems and issues that presently confront counselors.

These case studies are not fiction. They are faithful descriptions of real people living and working in a world the reader will recognize. The young people described are subject to the traumas that catch up with young people everywhere. However, steps have been taken to conceal the identities of the clients in order to preserve the confidentiality of the counseling relationship, and none of the individuals represented in the photographs is the actual person described in the case study.

Writing these case studies was a refreshing reminder to us that everyone is complex. If you think a person has only one or two dimensions, that is a reflection of your own lack of perception. If you will explore and probe the facades that people present, you will discover much more. All people are attractive in their efforts to find out who they are; the real challenge is to find out how we can help others complete this process.

In gathering this collection of case studies we have had the able assistance of many colleagues, counseling psychologists, school counselors, graduate students, and friends. We are greatly indebted to them for professional advice and service. However, our greatest debt is to the many clients who, by being themselves, have helped us to write this book about human behavior.

J.M.
J.M.

Counseling Psychology

Introduction:
The Case Study Method

Individual perceptions of the external world cause each of us to be different. Our sense of reality and personal values are greatly determined by the way in which we interpret what we see and how we think others view our behavior. In this sense, no two people are alike. The following vignette illustrates the principle: Razha, a Pakistani diplomat newly arrived in New York City, decided to visit an American coffee shop. The waitress took his order for a cup of tea and quickly placed before him a cup of boiling water and the usual string-bound tea bag. Razha proceeded to rip open the tea bag and spill out the contents into the cup of water. The waitress, amused by Razha's behavior, returned to his table to explain that the tea bag was made in such a manner as to let the flavor of the tea flow through the paper wrapping. Razha cheerfully thanked her and ordered a second cup of tea. When it arrived he was careful to place the tea bag in the cup of water. Not wanting to appear ungrateful or ignorant of the lesson he had just learned, Razha then ceremoniously placed four paper-wrapped packages of sugar in the tea cup. . . .

The preceding behavioral misadventure demonstrates the importance of being able to understand behavior from the frame of reference of the individual performing the behavior. Many counselors, regardless of their natural sensitivity to others or their training, rarely perceive how another person's problems can result in feelings of self-defeat and frustration. As we grow older, it becomes more difficult to look through the layers of protective scar tissue formed around our own ways of behaving. For example, we as adults forget how young people

1

actually feel. We can witness and describe how they react, but we seldom experience the freshness of the event. How, then, can we learn to view the world through the sensory antennae of our clients?

The psychological case study is a valuable method of studying the individual child or adolescent. Nowhere can one find the depth of feelings, the latitude for intuitive thinking and interpretation, and the true empathetic experience present in a case study. Few counselors would disagree with the notion that knowledge of a youth's personal goals, attitudes, and feelings should result in a more complete understanding of that young person. As Rothney (1968, p. 3) has indicated, "The good case study can give a meaningful total picture of the individual and, at the same time, throw light on details that were previously unclear."

The purpose for which a case study is written should determine its content and the form in which it is written. If the purpose of the individual study is to allow a teacher to understand the classroom behavior of a student, then biographical information, evidence of past academic performance, and anecdotal reports may be sufficient. However, if the counselor or therapist is attempting to deal with a deep-seated emotional disorder, other information regarding relationships in the home, peer influence, and social roles may be required. Each case study should be designed to help the reader understand the subject well enough to make effective plans toward resolution of areas of conflict.

The person reading the study should be able to understand the unique integration of personality characteristics motivating an individual's behavior. Just as a person's eyes and nose and mouth are differently put together so that his face becomes uniquely his own, so also are his basic thoughts and feelings differently put together to make his personality and his problems uniquely his own. If he can get to know the client and comprehend the context in which the disturbed behavior is taking place, then the reader's understanding will guide his counseling activity.

This means that understanding the client in his galaxy of problems often takes precedence over theory and technique. For example, a case study done on a black "juvenile delinquent" noted first that he had been arrested for stealing a basketball from a local sporting goods store. Subsequent information, revealed during a counseling session and recorded in the case study, indicated that he had stolen the basketball to give to his younger brother to keep him out of trouble. In this instance, the case study allowed the counselor to view several aspects of the youth's behavior simultaneously, thus receiving a more integrated understanding of his behavior. By identifying the motivating factors behind the theft, a reinterpretation of earlier behavior was possible. Another important aspect of the case study approach to understanding behavior is the vicarious experience offered to the reader. If the study is well written, the reader should come to feel as if he has shared, in some small way, a part of the anxiety and anguish which has caused the behavioral problem. The intent of the case study is to insert the counselor briefly into the "life space" of the client; such experiences should result in an increased understanding and awareness of the factors motivating client behavior.

This book is based on the belief that the reader will change his behavior as a result of contact with the people he comes to know in the following case studies. The combination of the reader's maturity and his experience with insights offered by case studies designed to encourage intuitive thinking and interpretation should result in increased professional awareness.

Kell and Mueller (1966) have indicated that when a client and counselor enter their relationship, both participants introduce into the relationship their total experience. The counselor enters the relationship with many attitudes that stem from different aspects of his experiences. The client brings into the counseling relationship his own conflicts which have arisen out of frustration in his previous interactions with other people. Throughout the counseling session the client and counselor share a reciprocal impact on the behavior of each other; they are both verbally and nonverbally trying to influence the behavior of each other.

It is important to consider the reciprocal nature of the relationship between the counselor and client. Some counselors still behave as if the problems of their clients can be solved through an external therapeutic approach. They assume that each difficulty can be isolated and defined, separated from the individual so as to lend itself to clear analysis, and then expect somehow to manipulate the appropriate behavioral variables for the proper solution. The key assumption is that counselors can act upon people while remaining fixed in their own behavior; they somehow expect to act like a hydraulic press that shapes metal but remains unaffected by the process. This is not possible. The major difficulties that confront counseling clients—violence, sexual mores, emotional disorders—are not easily solved. As the client and counselor work closely together to reach a solution, each gives of himself and participates in the experience. How can one partner remain unchanged?

3

The same is true of good case study material. As the reader reads the material, he begins to interact and participate in the study. Hypotheses about the motivation behind certain behavior are formulated, checked for validation, and then are tentatively accepted or discarded. The vicarious participation of the case study reader is similar to the active interaction between client and counselor.

Before proceeding to the case study material, a word of caution for the reader may be in order. As we counsel with individuals and learn how to heighten the capacity for self-understanding, we must recognize that we may also offer to our clients the tools by which they increase self-pity and self-delusion. We must be careful to remember that we all design our own lives as best we can and are responsible for whatever success or failure we fashion out of life. Every solution to personal problems is just that—personal. It does not come entirely from inside the client, nor from external sources, e.g., counselors imposing their will on the client. The solution comes most frequently from the interaction of the two.

How well do you understand your closest friends and loved ones? Perhaps not as well as you think you do. If you have recently experienced an emotional crisis situation (divorce, auto accident, severe illness, or death of a loved one) which forced you *really* to understand the behavior of another person, you might recognize how difficult it is. Each person we know is a unique and very complex individual trying to understand the world as best he can; it is not easy to accept another's perceptual frame of reference. Learning about the behavior of emotional and anxious people and trying to predict future behavior is a never-ending task. Changing human behavior in an effort to solve emotional problems through self-understanding is even more difficult. The following case studies present people in crisis situations, describing their struggle for a sense of direction and purpose in life. Will you accept the challenge to understand them?

BIBLIOGRAPHY: INTRODUCTION

Kell, B. L. and Mueller, W. J. *Impact and Change: A Study of Counseling Relationships.* New York: Appleton-Century-Crofts, 1966.
Rothney, J. M. *Methods of Studying the Individual Child: The Psychological Case Study.* Waltham, Mass.: Blaisdel Publishing Co. 1968.

4

I

Children

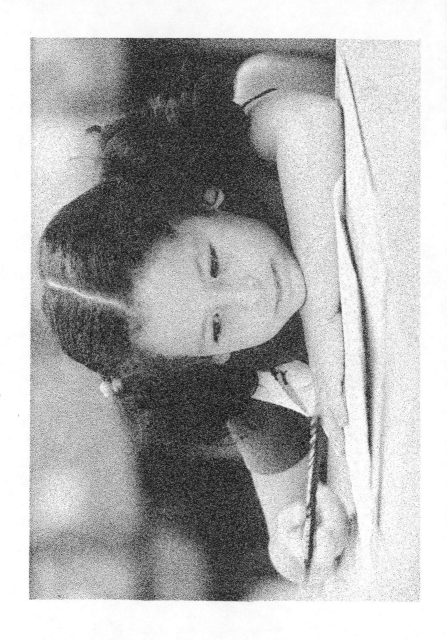

Cara

The teacher could feel herself giving in to frustration and hopelessness as she watched the small girl in the front row. The rest of the first grade class was eagerly involved in a spelling lesson, but Cara was twisting her pretty hair between her fingers and daydreaming. As her teacher watched, Cara let out a small sigh and gently laid her head on her arms. The teacher thought to herself, "I just don't understand it. I've tried to give her extra help, but she just doesn't seem to catch on. I know she's trying, and I know she's not dumb. I just don't know . . . maybe it's me." Finally, the teacher turned to Cara and spoke sharply, "Now, come on, Cara, get your head up and pay attention or you'll never get it right!"

This tragic scene is played out many times each year in elementary school classrooms. Many students with learning problems can be properly identified as having minimal brain dysfunction. Unfortunately, the student's problem often remains unidentified until the child has experienced academic failure and, in turn, developed feelings of inadequacy. The following case study concerns a seven-year-old girl who was suspected to have minimal brain dysfunction or, to use the popular term, a learning disability.

BACKGROUND

Cara is a small, brown-haired, wide-eyed little girl who often wears pigtails and an eager smile. From her physical appearance, Cara seems as happy and healthy as her playmates busily scurrying around on the playground. Indeed, she shouts and jumps with glee more often than many of her friends. But Cara is different. She is seven years old and in the first grade, but cannot tie her own shoes or button her coat. Cara has great difficulty in remembering where she puts things and has an unusually short attention span. Her problem today, if you were to ask her, would be: "I can't catch the ball good. The kids are always making fun of me."

After recent testing and a diagnostic interview with Cara, the school psychologist concluded that she has a perceptual learning disability which causes her to see things differently from the way her classmates see them. The psychologist requested a parent-teacher conference to discuss the test results and implications.

Cara is the only child of a young, college-educated, middle-class couple. Her father, age thirty-one, is employed as a claims adjuster for the local branch of a national insurance company. Her mother, age thirty, graduated from college with an elementary teaching degree and had completed a successful year of teaching when she became pregnant. Cara was the product of a full-term pregnancy and was easily delivered by her mother in the local hospital. Her birth was a welcome event to both parents.

During Cara's first year of life, little medical attention was needed other than the normal preventive injections. However, when Cara was two years old, she contracted a severe virus infection which caused her to have extremely high temperatures for several days. When Cara was three, she had corrective surgery for a kidney malfunction. The operation was quite delicate for such a young child and required a prolonged convalescence of two weeks in the hospital followed by several months of enforced bed rest at home. Her mother indicated that by age four, Cara had begun to experience headaches, dizziness, and marked lapses in her ability to focus her attention for more than a short period of time.

Evidence of concern surfaced when her mother gave Cara a reading readiness test she had learned about in one of her college classes. The test required the child to copy a circle, a square, and a triangle. Cara drew the circle, but couldn't copy the triangle. She became frustrated and anxious when she attempted to copy the square and began crying. Cara also had difficulty in learning social skills; when other children approached her, she shrieked loudly and cried for her mother.

When Cara entered the first grade the teacher noticed that she had an unusually short attention span and a low frustration level. She was upset easily and resorted to crying or withdrawal as coping mechanisms. Sometimes Cara preferred to use her right hand, while at other times she completed manual tasks with her left hand. She also had trouble learning to print. She frequently reversed such letters as *b*, *d*, and *q*. When Cara writes, her letters are mostly illegible shapes. When she does arithmetic, the answers are usually incorrect, with numbers transposed. The teacher discussed the problem with Cara's mother at a PTA meeting, and their combined observations underscored the idea that Cara needed special attention.

AREAS OF CONFLICT

A note from the teacher brought Cara to the counselor's attention. The teacher asked the counselor to visit her room to observe Cara's behavior during spelling class and suggested the need for psychological testing. After observing Cara's classroom behavior and conducting an initial interview with her, the counselor requested a diagnostic evaluation by the school psychologist. Cara was seen at the guidance center on two occasions for psychological evaluation. The psychologist noted that Cara was "cooperative but inattentive as she became restless and increasingly anxious during the testing sessions."

The following psychological tests were administered: Wechsler Intelligence Scale for Children (WISC), Wide Range Achievement Test (WRAT), Bender Visual Motor Gestalt (BG), and Illinois Test of Psycholinguistic Abilities (ITPA). The different test scores are presented in summary form in Table 1 to provide data for comparison purposes.

On the WISC verbal tests, Cara achieved her highest score in vocabulary (14) and lowest in arithmetic (7). The low arithmetic score was related to Cara's inability to count the blocks or to return the correct number of blocks to the test administrator. Her general range of information and her cumulative verbal learning ability were above average for children of her age.

Cara's scores on the WISC performance tests suggested visual motor deficiencies. She achieved scaled scores of 10 in picture completion and 9 in object assembly, thus indicating average functioning in visual closure and awareness of environmental detail; however, her scaled score on block design dropped to 6, indicating possible visual motor problems. The significant difference (23 points) between IQ scores on the

TABLE 1. *Test Achievement Record*

Student: Cara _____ Administered by: Mrs. _____, Psychologist

Date Tested: _____ Age of Child: **7/4** _____

Weschler Intelligence Scale for Children (WISC)

Verbal Tests	(scaled score)	*Performance Tests*	(scaled score)
Information	13	Picture completion	10
Comprehension	10	Picture arrangement	9
Arithmetic	7	Block design	6
Similarities	12	Object assembly	9
Vocabulary	14	Coding	5
Sum	56	Sum	41

Verbal IQ = 108　　　Performance IQ = 85　　　Full Scale IQ = 96

Date Tested: _____ Age of Child: **7/4** _____

Wide Range Achievement Test (WRAT)

Grade-level achievement　Standard score

Reading	Kindergarten	.8	79
Spelling	Kindergarten	.6	76
Arithmetic	First Grade	1.0	82

Date Tested: _____ Age of Child: **7/4** _____

Illinois Test of Psycholinguistic Abilities (ITPA)

Mean of standardization sample = 36　Cara's test score Median = 28

	Scaled score	*Age score*
Auditory Reception	34	6–10
Visual Reception	28	6– 0
Visual Sequential Memory	18	3– 4
Auditory Association	35	7– 0
Auditory Sequential Memory	28	4–10
Visual Association	15	4– 0

TABLE 1. Test Achievement Record —Continued

	Scaled score	Age score
Verbal Expression	40	8– 4
Visual Closure	18	4– 0
Grammatic Closure	35	7– 0
Manual Expression	20	3– 8

verbal and performance portions of the WISC underscored the probability of a learning disability for Cara.

The WRAT test scores offered evidence that Cara had not achieved well in academic areas. Her arithmetic scores on the WRAT and WISC tests indicated below average numerical skills. The BG test results suggested visual motor coordination difficulty. The psychologist indicated that this problem became quite evident when Cara had difficulty manipulating the pencil while attempting to complete the required drawings. Cara became upset when she made a mistake; she erased and redrew many of the designs and recounted the dots many times.

The ITPA test scores provided a comprehensive picture of Cara's auditory and visual skills. She achieved significantly low scores in four important categories: visual sequential memory, visual association, visual closure, and manual expression. Cara's scores on the verbal expression subtest were above average for her median score. The test data indicated that Cara had special learning problems related to spatial and motor tasks such as putting together puzzles or noticing the missing parts of pictures. Cara often became confused when she had to rely on her visual perception and memory.

After a thorough review of the test data, the teacher and counselor began to explore the implications of Cara's learning disability. She had displayed many symptoms and behaviors of a child with minimal brain dysfunction described by Clements (1968):

1. Average intellectual ability (WISC scores)
2. Specific learning disabilities (ITPA scores, teacher observation)
3. Perceptual deficits (ITPA scores)
4. Hypoactive, with high tolerance for failure (classroom behavior)
5. Short attention span (noted by teacher and psychologist).
6. Fine muscle coordination deficit (ITPA, BG scores)

Cara did not relate well to her classmates. A sociogram given by her teacher indicated that none of the classmates had listed Cara as a friend. Cara had listed two girls who sat near her. The teacher concluded that her classmates saw Cara as somewhat of a nuisance because of frequent tearful episodes between Cara and other children. As one student put it: "She cries a lot and won't help on projects. She's bad a lot."

It was true. Cara often withdrew from all class activity and entered into her fantasy world. When questioned about the content of her daydream world by the teacher, Cara responded:

> *Sometimes I think about meeting a close friend that will stay with me . . . sometimes nothing. When kids find out I can't do my work they make fun. They're always teasing me. That's mean. I try hard as I could. . . .*

Arrangements were made for Cara's parents to meet with the school counselor, psychologist, and teacher to discuss Cara's poor academic performance. The goals of the inital session with her parents were to communicate concern for Cara and to demonstrate the counselor's willingness to work with her. The counselor also wanted to explore the possibility of acting on the school psychologist's recommendation that Cara be placed in a learning disability classroom.

The interview began badly. Cara's parents were given the test results and a brief diagnostic summary which suggested the likelihood of a learning disability. As the psychologist and the counselor attempted to clarify the test score meanings, both parents quickly became defensive and refused to accept test score implications. The emotional tone of the conference was captured in a comment made later by Cara's mother:

> *The bitterest and most heart-wrenching words my husband and I ever heard were from the psychologist and counselor at Cara's school. They told us: "Cara has a learning disability problem." My first reaction was shock, followed by denial. We knew that Cara was having difficulty at school but we never suspected she was physically or psychologically defective.*
>
> *It was an awful realization for me as a mother. I know it sounds selfish, but when you have a pretty daughter, you think how she will be a cheerleader . . . or that she will be very popular and maybe someday we could enroll her in college. When they told us that Cara might have minimal brain dysfunction, it was*

*like saying that her future was canceled. Larry and I couldn't
believe it. . . .*

Fortunately, after an hour of tearful consideration and guarded
discussion, Cara's mother expressed her relief that at least something
was being done about Cara's "problem." She had watched Cara become
increasingly absorbed in her fantasy-daydream world and didn't know
what to do. She recognized Cara's lack of coordination and inability to
remember things and was ashamed of her crying in the classroom. Her
mother said that she hoped Cara would catch up and develop like other
children as she grew older, but she could see that Cara was falling further behind.

The school psychologist stressed four important advantages of placing Cara in the learning disability class: (1) a specially trained teacher,
(2) experiences designed for individual students, (3) class size restricted
to ten students, and (4) nongraded evaluation. She emphasized the idea
that the learning experiences would be varied, but each one would be
planned to help Cara to overcome her learning difficulty. Cara's parents
were to make the decision. The first conference ended on a cordial
note; teacher, counselor, and parents agreed that Cara could *learn.* They
decided to meet again to investigate specific things each of them could
do to help Cara lessen her learning problem.

Cara's mother called the counselor during the week to give parental
approval for placing Cara in the learning disability class. She asked for
an opportunity to meet with the new teacher prior to Cara's classroom
transfer. During the second parental conference, the counselor expressed a desire to enter a counseling relationship emphasizing behavioral counseling techniques with Cara. The counselor briefly explained
how learning theory served as the basis for behavioral counseling:

> *Based upon the assumption that behavior is lawful and deter-
> mined by antecedent events, behavioral counseling attempts to
> explain behavior problems in learning terms and then develop
> strategies for behavior change based upon the principles of
> learning.*
>
> *We can use a similar strategy for Cara. In this situation it is
> important to remember that behavioral counseling places great
> emphasis upon the recognition of personal anxiety as a precipita-
> tor of counseling problems. Anxiety in learning situations is the
> central explanatory concept for behavioral modification counsel-*

ing; if Cara is anxious, she can't learn. A corollary assumption is that she cannot be anxious and relaxed at the same time.

Our job is to learn how to offer Cara positive reinforcement for appropriate behavior in high-anxiety situations and thus increase her frequency of "good" behavior. Positive reinforcement is a stimulus that elicits or maintains desirable behavior; it can take the form of money, attention, praise, smiles, food, etc.

The counselor added that behavior modification techniques were not limited to the use of positive reinforcement. A counselor, teacher, or parent could also make use of modeling techniques, role-playing simulation games, and counterconditioning. Behavioral counseling techniques have been demonstrated to be effective with children exhibiting problems similar to Cara's, eliminating unproductive classroom behavior (Zimmerman, 1965) and improving academic performance (Scoresby, 1969). The counselor concluded her discussion of behavior modification counseling by outlining five important procedural steps in the process:

1. Problem assessment
2. Goal selection
3. Contingency analysis
4. Sequential training
5. Goal evaluation

Cara's parents and the learning disability teacher agreed to try behavior modification techniques to help Cara. They began by working on problem assessment. Cara's father suggested that the basic problem was her possible learning disability and anxiety about not being able to "do things like other kids." Her teacher added that Cara needed specific help to develop social skills; she couldn't go through school by whimpering and avoiding other children.

Goal selection for Cara was a difficult task. She seemed to have many interrelated problems. Her mother indicated that a realistic goal would be that she understand her learning limitations and develop one or two close friendships. Her father felt that a basic change in Cara's self-concept was necessary. He described Cara's cyclical self-defeating behavior:

She says or thinks, "I can't do that." When she tries something and fails, she's proven herself right. Each time she tries and fails at something and then retreats into tears, she's worse off. If she goofs up in class, the other kids make fun of her. That's double bad for her. No wonder she daydreams.

It was important to identify specific behavioral goals so that progress toward those goals could be monitored. Some form of criteria would have to be devised to measure Cara's progress toward a better self-concept and the adoption of social skills. The counselor expressed concern that Cara should help to decide her goals for counseling. They agreed that Cara was to be given an opportunity to discuss her goals for counseling during the first interview with the counselor.

The contingency analysis process focused on creating a hierarchy or reward system to reinforce Cara when she behaved appropriately. The operant learning process stressed the importance of giving positive reinforcement immediately after desirable behavior has taken place. By creating a reinforcement menu for Cara, the adults could selectively reinforce Cara's good behavior and not offer her reinforcement for inappropriate behavior. It was hypothesized that, by systematically pairing anxiety producing situations (getting to know new classmates) with immediate positive reinforcement (candy, recognition, and praise) for appropriate behavior (playing with another child), Cara could become less anxious and develop more adequate behavior.

The implementation of sequential training was to follow the creation of a "not difficult" to "difficult" hierarchy of personal and social activities for Cara. Her parents and counselor agreed that the teacher was most qualified to design the remediation techniques and learning experiences that would offer opportunities for deliberate and systematic reinforcement. She offered to carefully observe Cara's present classroom behavior and to make up a checklist of her activities related to social skills and personal behavior. The observation information would describe baseline activities that should or should not be reinforced by the teacher and provide a frame of reference for what activities Cara found rewarding.

The role of Cara's parents in sequential training was to supplement the teacher's and the counselor's efforts. By spending a part of each school evening with Cara, participating in simulation games designed to elicit social skills, her parents would be able to reinforce those skills. They recognized that the amount of reinforcement offered to Cara during school hours was minor when compared to the amount of reinforcement they could give Cara in their home. Their efforts were to focus on helping Cara learn that she was a good person with limited skills; they would try to withhold attention from her when she cried or played the game "poor little me." When Cara completed something successfully, her parents agreed to reward her with a pleasant experience.

The counselor's role was to coordinate the behavior modification efforts of parents and teacher, as well as to provide Cara with an opportunity for behavioral counseling in her office for an hour each week.

Parents, teacher, and counselor decided that the goal evaluation process could be accomplished by having Cara's parents and teacher complete behavioral observations and anecdotal reports at four-week intervals. Their objective descriptions of Cara's behavior changes would provide important feedback regarding the effectiveness of the reinforcement activities.

When the second parental conference ended, the sense of frustration and failure for Cara's parents had been transformed into a concrete plan of behavior modification.

INITIAL COUNSELING INTERVIEW

The counselor began the first counseling session by explaining to Cara that her mother and teacher had asked her to visit with Cara about changing to the new classroom and teacher. She told Cara that she wanted to help her like the new teacher and make it easier to know some of the new boys and girls. Then she asked Cara an open-ended question: "How do you feel about yourself today?" The silence in the room grew for a moment and then Cara tentatively responded, "My thumb hurts."

Cara gazed intently into the counselor's eyes, as if she were somehow measuring how much she could trust this new lady. Then she slowly extended her sore thumb for the counselor to examine. The physical touch of the counselor's hands upon Cara's injured thumb seemed to create a bond of mutual trust. Her counselor sensed that Cara could not express her emotions verbally; touch and trust were to play an important part in the counseling relationship.

The counselor continued the session by saying that she would like to do some counseling with Cara to help her solve her adjustment problems at school. Cara was confused about the purpose of counseling and asked:

16

Is it only for dumb kids like me? Most of school isn't any fun. Why does teacher try and make me work so hard? I wish she would stop picking on me.

Cara began to cry softly. Her counselor chose to pay little attention to her tears and began to talk about the purpose of counseling visits. The counselor explained that they would talk about specific classroom problems and also discuss other things like not having any close friends, crying when she felt bad, or any problem that Cara thought was important. As Cara listened to her counselor, she stopped crying.

In developing her relationship with Cara, the counselor carefully pointed out Cara's responsibility for participation and the setting of counseling goals. Cara thought about what her counselor said during five quiet moments. Then she indicated that important goals for her would be "to feel better in school" and to be able to put her own clothes on. Making a new friend in her new class was also important. She said:

I get mixed up a lot. Teacher says I'm confused. When they laugh at my mistakes, I feel kinda sick and cry a lot. Sometimes I dream about runnin' away from this school, far, far away. . . .

The most important thing accomplished during the first counseling session was that Cara began to view her counselor as a friend who could help her. The counselor wanted to help Cara describe how she would like to feel or achieve in the future, as compared with her present unpleasant behavior and feelings. By creating a relationship in which Cara identified her goals and priorities, the counselor was able to select effective reinforcement methods related to Cara's personal problems. The first interview ended when the counselor asked Cara if she wanted to come back for more counseling next week. Cara simply said, "OK," and left the office.

COUNSELING METHODOLOGY

Two important steps in the behavior modification process, problem assessment and goal selection, had been completed prior to the second counseling session. The contingency analysis procedures were implemented when the learning disability teacher constructed a checklist of sixteen of Cara's academic and social behaviors during the previous week:

resting head on desk	18	participation—storytime	2
using paints	3	playing with others	1
acting helpless	24	crying—arguments	26
silent withdrawal	11	assembling block designs	3
using colored pencils	5	cooperation with others	2
reading silently	2	writing lesson	3
losing work materials	12	getting drink	12
drawing on board	4	reviewing spelling words	7

As the counselor and the teacher reviewed the checklist, it became obvious that Cara frequently demonstrated inappropriate behavior related to the development of a positive self-attitude and adequate social skills. They agreed that the next objective was for the teacher to carefully and systematically offer Cara positive reinforcement for appropriate classroom behavior. The teacher agreed to use candy as a primary reinforcement, and praise and attention were to be used as conditioned reinforcements.

The selection of reinforcement contingencies for Cara's successful behavior was only a part of the contingency analysis process. The counselor pointed out that a basic principle of behavioral counseling is that reinforcement which immediately follows a desirable response is more effective than delayed reinforcement. The teacher understood that she was to pay careful attention to the timing of her reinforcement; it was to occur immediately after Cara successfully completed a behavior such as cooperating with her team on a class project.

The large number of incorrect social behaviors on the checklist was particularly important. They suggested to the counselor that modeling techniques might offer a shortcut to increasing Cara's favorable social behaviors. Exposure to the successful behavior of a peer-model would create the opportunity for Cara to imitate the model's behavior. When Cara's imitative behavior was completed, the teacher gave her immediate positive reinforcement. The teacher liked the model-reinforcement idea. She said that it would be fairly easy to encourage Cara to work with a girl named Sharon that Cara had shown interest in.

The second counseling session began with the same open-ended question: "How do you feel about yourself today, Cara?" Cara answered with information about the third grade science experiments with frogs. She wanted to talk about things that didn't have much to do with her problems. The counselor refocused her attention by asking directly about how she was doing in her efforts to make friends with her new classmates and teacher. Cara immediately began crying and stretched her arms out to her counselor. The counselor allowed Cara to climb up on her lap and cry for a while. Then she gently, but firmly, placed Cara back on her chair and asked her to tell about what was on her mind. Cara said she felt bad because she missed her old teacher. The new teacher spent more time with her and was friendly, but she missed the classroom where she had spent three-fourths of the school year.

The counselor encouraged Cara's expression of anxious feelings by systematically reinforcing her statements with words of direct approval such as, "I'm glad you told me how you feel." As Cara continued talking about her feelings, the counselor used indirect and more subtle reinforcements such as head nodding or the client-centered "Mm-humm." The dialogue offered below evidences the counselor's attempts to get Cara to identify specific behaviors she could do to solve some of her problems:

CR: Cara, can you think of anything we can do to solve one of
        your problems?
CARA: Well. . . . Uhhh, I guess I could try harder.
CR: Yes, that's a good idea. But that isn't really something specific
        that you can do. Can you think of a specific thing you could
        do to feel better?
CARA: Umm. . . . Do you mean like, uhh, like a tiny thing?
CR: Sort of. . . .
CARA: How about sitting in my chair with feet on the floor. Teacher
        wants me to do that. Is that a specific thing?
CR: Yes, that would be a good idea.
CARA: Or, maybe . . . maybe I could read lessons with my mom. She
        reads a lot when nobody is around. She sits on the couch with
        her feet up and drinks pop when she reads. I'd like that.
CR: That's a very good idea. She might like it if you could read at
        the same time. It would be like sharing something with her. A
        special time for the two of you. She could read her book and
        you could read one of yours.
CARA: But, humm, I make lots of mistakes. . . .
CR: [no response]
CARA: Well, that's all I can think of. . . . Can I go back to class?

The third counseling interview began on a very favorable note. Cara enthusiastically told her counselor that her mother had made some large, pretty sandpaper alphabet letters that stuck to the basement wall.

The pride Cara felt for "her letters" was obvious; she brought them to school for Show and Tell time. Cara's mother had called the counselor to alert her to the letters game she and her husband Larry had created. The rules were simple. Cara was to spell out with her letters a new word that she was interested in that day. The word that she spelled out on the wall was to be important to her and had to be spelled correctly. *Boy, girl, slow, ball, fish, cat, dog, mom,* and *dad* were her favorite words.

The fourth counseling session was similar to the third. Cara remained enthusiastic about working on spelling with her letters. She said her teacher had asked her to learn how to put her own coat on by carefully watching Sharon put hers on. Then Cara was to turn to the full-length mirror and put her coat on. If she buttoned all three buttons correctly, the teacher would give her a piece of candy. Cara said that she liked that!

Following the fourth week of counseling, Cara's parents and teacher completed anecdotal reports. Her mother wrote:

> *Every night Larry works with Cara and her alphabet. They make a game out of it. If she spells 10 words in a row correctly, she can have something nice. Ice cream cones or a bottle of pop are her favorite reinforcers.*
>
> *It is amazing how Larry, following the teacher's suggestions, is teaching Cara to read better. Night after night they work slowly together because he makes it fun for her and she is eager to learn for him. She is making great progress.*
>
> *My role has been to support Cara's reading activity. We have set aside a special reading time each night, just before she goes to bed. She sits on the couch with me and we relax and read together. She has her lesson books and I have my magazines. After we read for a while, we stop to talk with each other about the things we have read. We show each other the important things.*
>
> *I have really come to understand much better how Cara thinks about things. I am beginning to see the difficult challenges she faces when she takes on even simple tasks. We're much closer now. All three of us sense it.*

Cara's teacher reported noticeable success with behavioral modeling reinforcement efforts. She pointed out that it took a great deal of time to watch Cara so that she could time her reinforcement to occur immediately after Cara exhibited favorable behavior, but that her efforts seemed to be worthwhile. She wrote:

> *Your suggestion about using Sharon as a peer-model was a good one. For the past week I've had Sharon put her coat on and then button it up while Cara stood by and paid close attention. Then it was Cara's turn to stand in front of the full-length mirror and do the same thing.*

> *I gave Cara a lot of attention and praise when she approximated the right behavior. When she gave up and cried, I told Sharon to discontinue and then paid little attention to Cara. (That wasn't easy.) After only four days of practice Cara could button all three buttons on her own coat! She was so proud of herself. Now we are working on learning how to tie her own shoes. She and Sharon seem to have struck up a tentative friendship.*

By the seventh counseling interview, many changes had taken place in Cara's character. Cara was much more expressive in her counseling sessions. She began by saying that she was looking forward to the end of the school year, but that she would miss some of the things she was doing in school. She said that her new teacher was helping her to work with suppressed alphabet letters which could teach her how to print different words. Cara liked that. The following dialogue between Cara and her counselor illustrates the dynamics of their counseling relationship:

CR: *You seem to like school better now. Can you tell me about it?*

CARA: *Well, uhhh. . . . It's just better. My new teacher is nice and I can do some of the things in there. I've been working with Sharon to get better. Teacher says we can work together. She's smart.*

CR: *That's good.*

CARA: *But, well, sometimes I cry. I don't know why, but I still do. I feel awful bad when I can't do some things. Johnny Cites makes noises and then the other kids laugh at me. Then I feel dumber than ever.*

CR: *I'm glad you told me that. It's not fun to feel bad, is it. . . ?*

CARA: *No. But things aren't bad like they were. Teacher's been getting after me lately when I start daydreaming. Sometimes I forget where I put my work things.*

21

CR: That's good that you don't cry as much. Do you feel better
        when you don't cry?
CARA: Sometimes I do.

Following the eighth counseling session, a parental conference was called to complete the goal evaluation process. Cara's teacher made use of the previous behavior checklist to gain objective evidence to support her subjective feelings about Cara's marked progress. The results are offered below:

resting head on desk	6	participation—storytime	8
using paints	7	playing with others	10
acting helpless	10	crying—arguments	5
silent withdrawal	6	assembling block designs	7
using colored pencils	5	cooperating with others	11
reading silently	11	writing lesson	8
losing work materials	6	getting drink	7
drawing on board	8	reviewing spelling words	12

It was clear that Cara had made progress in her social skills in the classroom.

Cara's teacher added that the most important change in Cara's behavior was the adoption of an attitude of cooperation with others. She was participating in class activities much more now, and her daydreaming periods had decreased significantly. Her teacher summarized with the comment:

Cara is responding well to the behavioral counseling and teaching methods. Most of her behavior change is related to her new attitude about herself and her mistakes. She seems to accept her limitations better and is much less easily frustrated. Recently she went a whole day without a single tear. Her parents' cooperation and work at home with reading and spelling games make a big difference.

Cara's parents agreed. They had witnessed the changes in her behavior and were quite pleased. They would continue to play reading and spelling games with Cara during the summer months so that she would not lose her interest in school activities. At the teacher's suggestion, they had signed Cara up for summer swimming lessons to provide visual-motor coordination experiences.

OUTCOME

The world of a child with a learning disability is usually one of many limits—those smotheringly imposed by parents who want only to help their child and those real limitations which are brought about by the child's lowered level of mental functioning. Both kinds of limitations present psychological handicaps to the normal pathways of learning. In this case, Cara was fortunate because her parents were willing to cooperate with the school counselor and learning disability teacher. Cara made a much better social adjustment in the noncompetitive academic atmosphere of the learning disability classroom. Her specially trained teacher could devote more attention to her individual learning difficulties. Cara terminated her ninth and last counseling session with her counselor by saying, "I did reach a counseling goal. I made you my very first teacher-lady friend. Goodbye."

FOCUS QUESTIONS

1. Can you think of an alternative counseling theory or methodology for this case? Why do you think it would be effective?
2. Counselors have long recognized that new insights into normal, healthy development of children can be gained from the study of exaggerated behavior that occurs in atypical individuals. Does this behavior modification case support that notion? How?
3. Can you recommend two important ways the school system and counselors could work to meet the needs of children with learning problems who possess different achievement levels?

BIBLIOGRAPHY: CARA

Clements, Sam. *Some Aspects of the Characteristics, Management, and Education of the Child with Learning Disabilities.* Little Rock: Arkansas Association for Children with Learning Disabilities, 1968.

Scoresby, A. Lynn. "Improving Academic Performance." In Krumboltz, John D., and Thoreson, Carl E., eds. *Behavioral Counseling: Cases and Techniques.* New York: Holt, Rinehart and Winston, 1969.

Zimmerman, E. H., and Zimmerman, J. "The Alteration of Behavior in a Special Classroom Situation." In Ullmann, Leonard P., and Krasner, Leonard, eds. *Case Studies in Behavior Modification.* New York: Holt, Rinehart and Winston, 1965.

CRITIQUE OF THE CASE OF CARA

The choice of behavior modification techniques as the basic mode of treatment in the case of Cara seems quite appropriate just so long as one realizes that relationship is probably the most significant variable affecting the success or failure of these techniques. Perhaps the most potent factor involved in the treatment of Cara was the close coopera-tion among the significant others in Cara's treatment program. It would be difficult as well as unwise to attribute Cara's progress to teacher, school psychologist, counselor, child-model, or parents alone. The fact that all worked closely toward relatively clearly defined goals was criti-cal to their success.

Even though behavior modification was an appropriate treatment mode for Cara, there are a few points to consider if one wishes to spec-ulate on an *ideal* treatment program for Cara. Since Cara had difficulty relating to her peer group, structured play group therapy may have been preferred to individual therapy, provided that the group was small—perhaps only two or three children—and had one child at least who could serve as a model for Cara. Perhaps a combination of struc-tured individual and structured group play therapy would have been preferred over individual therapy. Structure and consistency would likely be important elements in the success of any treatment plan for Cara.

Secondly, it is a questionable procedure to place any person in a homogeneous group continuously and for extended time periods. A problem child or adult who has deficits of an emotional, physical, or intellectual character, when placed with others with the same deficits, has no "healthy" models with whom to identify. It is therefore impor-tant that Cara be given many opportunities to relate to normal children during her school day so that she does not adjust to a learning disability child's role.

Also related to the counseling intervention chosen were the number and frequency of counselee sessions. One hour once a week would not be as potent as two or three shorter periods spaced throughout the week. More than nine sessions would likely be necessary with Cara, time permitting.

The counselor's behavior was not always consistent with the plan to eliminate nonadaptive behavior. For example, she systematically rein-forced anxious statements of the counselee. At times, the counselor was also too vague. Telling Cara in the first session that "she would like to do some counseling with Cara to help her solve her adjustment problems at school" was a poor explanation, for a seven year old, of what counseling is.

A more comprehensive behavioral approach to Cara would include setting up a program to deal with all of her modalities where deficits existed. Using a plan such as Lazarus' (1974) multimodal model, intervention strategies could have been developed to work more directly on Cara's physical coordination, although a partial plan was used to help her master buttoning her coat and tying her shoes. Nothing was done directly either with her fantasy life (imagery) nor her cognitive deficits related to self-defeating thinking. No mention was made of any kind of physical examination or the possible need for chemotherapy. Nevertheless, the program developed for Cara was more complete than for most school counseling cases and involved the concurrent efforts in treatment of the significant others in Cara's life. Since Cara's problems were being attacked from several vantage points, the treatment program represents a relatively good model for the school setting.

Discussion Questions

1. Contrast the approach that a psychoanalytically oriented therapist would have used with Cara versus the behavior modification approach. Which approach do you consider most relevant?
2. Using your own approach, simulate an individual counseling session with Cara during the first interview. Include a description of what counseling is, what would be expected of her and you, and how counseling might help Cara.

Bibliography: Critique of Cara

Lazarus, Arnold A. "Multimodal Behavior Therapy in Groups." In Gazda, George M., ed. *Basic Approaches to Group Psychotherapy and Group Counseling,* Second Edition. Springfield, Ill.: Charles C Thomas, 1974.

Charles

Charles doesn't come from a broken home—he hides there. For several weeks he has threatened to "end the hassle and mess" of his young life by dropping from the highway bridge near the school. Yesterday he carried out his threat. Luckily, he survived the drop with minor cuts and bruises which openly evidenced his desperate mental situation.

This morning, Charles was asked to come to the counselor's office to discuss what happened before school yesterday. He entered the office with his head hung low, as if guilty of something he shouldn't have done. He quietly took a chair and focused his attention on his hands as he tied and untied knots in a piece of string. Charles is small and slight for his eleven years; his clothing is worn and faded, yet neat.

The counselor began with an open-ended question: "Can you tell me what happened yesterday morning, Charles?" A long silence followed. Then in a rush of words, Charles said, "I come to school early, but it was locked. So I went down by the bridge before anyone else was around. Then some other kids come along. I climbed up on the guardrail and looked down for a while, and then I just let go."

BACKGROUND

Charles lives in a small, meagerly furnished house located in the center of an urban black ghetto. The house is neglected and shows aging from weather. A rusty fence encloses two beat-up, junked cars and an old washing machine in the backyard. A discarded moss-ridden couch dominates the sagging porch area as if to intimidate visitors. Charles stays with his sixty-seven-year-old maternal grandmother and his mentally retarded uncle, age thirty-two. His grandmother receives old age assistance, Social Security benefits and government commodities. Charles shares a double bed with his uncle except when his uncle is having a "bad" night, then Charles is forced to sleep on the floor.

Charles's mother was eighteen years old when he was born. She implies that she had been trapped into marriage by her pregnancy and sought release from her marriage when Charles was about a year old. The divorce was granted and his mother retained legal custody of Charles. His mother further dissociated herself from marital responsibility and possible guilt feelings by placing Charles in the home of her aged mother and moving to another section of the neighborhood. After experiencing several years of "freedom," Charles's mother remarried and presently has two daughters, ages eight and six, in her new home. Her second husband will not accept the responsibility of caring for Charles. Charles is not welcome in the new family home because he is the son of another man.

The child-rearing practices of Charles's grandmother do not work out very well. His grandmother explains, "It was enough I had to do to keep me and my grown son alive. I couldn't go running around looking for Charles to keep him out of trouble, because I haven't been well myself for a long time." Charles spent most of his early childhood years roaming in the neighborhood in search of someone to play with and something to eat. By default, Charles experienced little adult company or close supervision until he entered school.

During the first grade, Charles made a remarkable effort to adjust to the structured atmosphere of school. His female teacher made the following observation:

> *Charles is trying very hard in school. He is reading nicely in the second pre-primer, but needs to calm down and concentrate more. He could do much better if he would use more self-control and not seek instant gratification of his desires. Charles wants and needs a great deal of my attention and love, as if he is deprived from similar attention at home. He requires a large amount of praise; he always says, "I can't do it." Then he is very excited and pleased when he discovers he really* can *do it.*

Further anecdotal records indicated that Charles was very sensitive about his status with other children in first grade. He actively cultivated the friendship of certain peers and savagely defended his position as group leader with physical assaults on the other children to keep them in line.

In the second and third years of school, Charles continued to develop stronger antisocial behaviors. He was the most active and fidgety boy in the room, always ready to divert the teacher's attention to himself. Somewhat typical of a child faced with a great deal of anxiety, Charles occasionally told lies to avoid punishment and escape reprimands. His third grade teacher wrote:

> *Charles has a very severe temper. He is easily irritated and can change his mood in an instant. He goes as far as he can to keep from minding me; I am beginning to think that he enjoys punishment because of the attention he gets. Charles is a poor loser in playground games and hasn't developed social skills. For him, everything is settled with fists. He continues to make funny facial motions in a clownish manner and distracting noises during class hours.*

Charles is currently in the fifth grade and has made little progress in developing personal social skills. His need for acceptance is still vented by immediate action and physical touch. His fifth grade teacher notes that Charles has recently become almost intolerable in the classroom. She has requested an evaluation of Charles by the Psychological Services Unit of the public schools for possible placement in the classroom for emotionally disturbed students. She writes:

> *Charles is extremely active and is unable to make an adjustment in a regular classroom situation. He moves around the room constantly and draws back his hand to challenge a fight instantly. He feels a need to touch or hit everyone in the room, including me. Charles takes children's books, pencils, etc., in an effort to increase attention to himself. Charles resists classroom structure and organization. His lack of concentration interferes with completion of his lessons. He greatly enjoys being in close physical contact with adults and seeks the companionship of boys much older than he is.*

AREAS OF CONFLICT

Charles has many interrelated behavioral problems. One of the most important areas of conflict is his overwhelming need for attention and affection. His behaviors of clowning, teasing, hitting other children, and disrupting organized activities in the classroom seem to be directly

TABLE 2. Test Achievement Record

Student: Charles*	Completed by: Mrs. X, school psychologist

Date: *Lee Clark Reading Readiness Test*, Kindergarten-First grade Chronological age: 6 yr. 3 mo. Grade placement: 1 yr. 1 mo. Raw scores: Letter symbols, *8*; Concepts 7; Word symbols *0*; Total raw score *15*; Possible score *84*.
Test indications: Poor reading readiness, delay expectancy of 7 mo.

Date: *Metropolitan Achievement Test*
Chronological age: 8 yr. 4 mo. Grade placement: 3 yr. 2 mo.

	word knowledge	word discrimination	reading	spelling	language	arithmetic comprehension	arithmetic problems
Stanine	4	4	4	0	2	3	3
% ile	35	20	30	0	5	33	15

Date:

Stanine	1	2	1	2	inc.	inc.	inc.
% ile	1	5	4	5	inc.	inc.	inc.

Chronological age: 9 yr. 4 mo. Grade placement: 4 yr. 2 mo.

Date: *Metropolitan Reading Test*, Elementary Form B.
Chronological age: 9 yr. 10 mo. Grade placement: 4 yr. 8 mo.
Test results: Word knowledge, Grade evaluation: 2 yr. 6 mo.
                Reading skills, Grade evaluation: 2 yr. 0 mo.

Date: *California Test of Mental Maturity*
Chronological age: 10 yr. 6 mo. Grade placement: 5 yr. 4 mo.

	language	nonlanguage	Total
Stanine	3	3	3
% ile	16	16	14

Date: *Comprehensive Test of Basic Skills*
Chronological age: 11 yr. 3 mo. Grade placement: 5 yr. 0 mo.

	reading vocabulary	reading comprehension	language	arithmetic comprehension	arithmetic concept	arithmetic application	study skills
Stanine	1	1	1	1	2	3	1
% ile	1	1	2	2	5	13	2

*retained in fifth grade

related to this need. Charles's lack of success in school is well documented by his failing grades and poor scores on the group tests that he has taken during his five years of school. The different test scores reported in Table 2 are represented in summary form to provide data for comparison purposes.

The results of the reading readiness test administered in the first grade indicated that Charles entered school deficient in reading skills. Test results from the Metropolitan Achievement Test, administered in the third grade, indicated that he demonstrated low-average achievement in four subtest areas: word knowledge, word discrimination, reading, and arithmetic computation. Charles was particularly deficient in spelling and language skills.

It is important to notice the significant differences between the scores achieved on the Metropolitan Achievement Test administered in the third and fourth grades. In several areas the test scores dropped from the fourth stanine to the first stanine, and Charles did not complete three subject areas. The test scores indicate that Charles had changed from the low-average category to the lower limits of the below-average category. The percentile scores also manifested an equally drastic drop, with the highest percentile being five.

The California Test for Mental Maturity, administered in the fifth grade, indicated that Charles continued to achieve at the below average level. The most recent test, the Comprehensive Test of Basic Skills, indicated very little cumulative academic achievement. Charles consistently scored in the below-average and poor categories in each subtest area.

A summary review of the test data would indicate that Charles began school with a limited repertoire of skills which would help him to perform adequately in school. He has been unable to correct those learning deficiencies and has gradually fallen further behind in his academic progress each year, although he has been advanced in grade placement. From the available data it is difficult to determine the cause(s) of his learning disability. The possibility of organic brain damage should not be ruled out; however, his impoverished cultural environment and lack of adult supervision and attention suggest plausible rationales for his inability to do well in school.

Chares's cumulative grade report (Table 3) closely parallels information found in the test results. His grades in the first three years of school were satisfactory, with two notable exceptions—reading and spelling. Charles was deficient in those related areas and received unsatisfactory grades. His best subjects were art, music, and social studies.

31

TABLE 3. *Elementary School Grades*

Student: Charles

Subject:	Grade Level				
	1	2	3	4	5
Arithmetic	S	S	S	U	F
Art	S	S	S	U	F
Language: Grammar	S	S	S	U	D
Music	S	S	S	U	F
Reading	U	U	U	U	F
Science	S	S	S	U	D
Social Studies	S	S	S	U	D
Spelling	U	U	U	U	F
Social Conduct	S	S	S	U	U
Days Absent	23	40	43	62	NI

A significant change occurred in Charles's grades during his fourth year in school. He received a succession of totally unsatisfactory report cards and he was absent from school much more frequently. Perhaps it was significant that Charles encountered his first male classroom teacher in the fourth grade. Because Charles demonstrated only minimal improvement in the fifth grade (new grading system employed), he was retained at the year's end.

A recent anecdotal comment from his present female teacher clarifies the motivation for some of his impulsive behavior:

> *Charles is unable to recognize or understand the needs of others. He has great difficulty in learning developmental tasks in growing up. An example: he gives others candy and loans them money, but when his demand for acceptance is not met, he beats them up. On the playground he uses vile, obscene words and then breaks into hysterical laughter . . . a few minutes later he begs to be taken into my arms.*

Much of Charles's behavior follows a cyclical pattern: increased anxiety in unfavorable situations, followed by impulsive inappropriate behavior (often an attack on the perceived source of his anxiety), followed by deep feelings of rejection and self-pity. Each time Charles experiences a self-defeating situation at school or home, he becomes more unhappy with himself and those around him. He then descends another small step on the downward psychological stairway leading to suicidal depression.

A second major area of conflict for Charles is the fragmented existence he lives at home. He is seldom held accountable for his behavior by his grandmother or uncle, and as a result he has received little adult supervision. What discipline he does receive is sporadic, and often the amount of physical punishment is out of proportion to the misbehavior involved.

The situation changes greatly, however, when his mother visits the home. As if she is trying to compensate for the many days she is gone from Charles, his mother usually overorganizes his activities when she visits. It is easy to predict the physical and emotional explosions that occur between Charles and his mother when she tries to restrict his behavior.

Charles has also indicated that his mother often makes negative comparisons between himself and his two half-sisters who live with her. She frequently says, "Why can't you be a good child like my Francine or Dottie? They always do good in school and don't give me any sass." The fact that his half-sisters go to the same school causes Charles many problems. He often pushes them and taunts them with obscene names. In retaliation the girls lie to their mother and exaggerate Charles's behavior.

INITIAL COUNSELING INTERVIEW

Charles was fortunate to have a sensitive black woman in her mid-thirties as his counselor. As she listened to him talk about the chain of unpleasant events that caused him to drop from the bridge, she tried to communicate feelings of warmth and unqualified acceptance. Charles talked about how he had taken a bright green T-shirt from the neighborhood Goodwill store on the preceding day. He told his friends that his father had returned home and given it to him as a present. Unfortunately, after Charles told his story to several friends, one remembered having seen the T-shirt on the store counter and could prove that Charles had stolen it. Rather than admit his guilt, Charles chose to fight the boy to defend his honor. He lost both.

Charles said that he went home from school early and received a broom-handle beating from his grandmother for scuffing up his clothes and fighting. As Charles sought refuge from two bad situations, he went to his secret hiding place where he could be by himself in an overturned car in a vacant lot. He decided to dig up his buried savings of $3.26 and run away from home. However, his mentally retarded uncle had found the hiding place and stolen the money. Charles spent the night in the car, sobbing to himself and desperately trying to find a way out of his sadness.

As Charles finished describing what happened to the counselor, his head slumped down, and he retreated to the posture of a defeated child. He looked at the piece of string again and slowly let it drop to the floor. The counselor recognized this moment as a critical time in the development of her relationship with Charles. She said, "The most important thing to me, Charles, is what you want to do. How you feel about yourself." It was quiet in the room for a long moment. Then Charles raised his head and focused his eyes squarely on those of his counselor. He whispered, "I dunno. . . . I just don't care no more, you understand. . . ." He hung his head again, and a tear dropped quietly to the floor. The counselor understood.

For the next ten minutes she tried to help Charles learn how he felt about himself. Then, in an abrupt change of mood, Charles began to laugh about how his act of dropping from the bridge had changed things. He said that the teachers and other kids "weren't messing with [him] anymore." The counselor began to suspect that the primary reason Charles dropped from the highway bridge was to get attention from his friends and teachers. The first counseling session ended when Charles and his counselor scheduled another session for that afternoon.

The counselor began the second counseling session by inviting Charles to visit a playroom on the second floor. As they walked up the steps, Charles took the counselor's hand and squeezed it tightly. The counselor opened the door and introduced Charles to the empty playroom by saying:

> It's not much, but it's a place where you can be yourself. You can be as big or small as you want to be. You can even do nothing if you want to.

Charles sighed, and the tightness and sadness seemed to lessen. His eyes began to explore the room. It was not attractive. There was a cold darkness in the room because of the poor lighting and lack of decoration. He could see a sink with running water and some small stools to sit on. The walls of the room were painted brown and yellow and showed evidence of someone's paint-splattered anger. The linoleum floor was blue-green specked and dirty. There were different kinds of toys on a small table, on the floor, and on the shelves around the room. A damaged dollhouse lay beside the table used for painting and shaping clay. There were many dolls—mamma dolls, pappa dolls, and brother and sister dolls. Some of the dolls were in good shape; others were horribly twisted and broken. The room smelled heavily of moist clay, stale watercolor paints, and drying glue. At the far end of the room was one large window that overlooked the school neighborhood. Charles was to learn later that, by standing on tiptoe, he could see his grandmother's house.

Eventually Charles let his eyes come to rest on a small black doll that represented a young boy. He walked into the playroom and picked it up. He looked into the doll's eyes for a long time and then he tucked it under his arm and sat down on a small chair facing the wall. The counselor entered the room and said, "You and I can spend an hour together in here today. You can play with any of the toys or whatever you want to." She sat down in the old overstuffed rocking chair placed conveniently inside the door and watched Charles. In a few moments, the boy stood up and began to pace around the room. After touching many of the different toys, he pulled a small stool up next to the counselor and faced her directly. He said that he wanted to make up a story about the small doll. He would make up the first half of the story and she would have to finish it. As Charles began to tell his story, the counselor knew he was trying to make a friend.

COUNSELING METHODOLOGY

One week later, the counselor reflected on her decision to work with Charles using play therapy. She said:

> *I knew Charles was mixed-up, serious. I wanted to let him know that someone cared, really cared, about him. Nothing was as important as getting him to feel like I was his friend. Everything else had to come after that.*
>
> *I could read the hurt in his face. He was too scared to try to reach down and understand his mixed-up feelings. My hunch was*

that he might find or do something in play therapy to hang on to, you know. Some way of getting rid of his loneliness and fear.

In that room I could give him some personal warmth without asking for something back. He could work things out at his own speed. Meanwhile he would have a place in the school where he felt safe.

Nondirective play therapy is based on the assumption that the child has within himself not only the ability to solve his problems satisfactorily but also the growth impulse which makes mature behavior more satisfying than immature behavior. Play is a child's natural way of investigating the world around him. Through play, the child re-creates what he observes in the world around him, as *he* sees it. His play activities are a graphic illustration of the child's relationships to others.

Play therapy is designed to give the child a chance to play out accumulated feelings of frustration, insecurity, confusion, and defeat. In the playroom, a child develops the skill of creating and becoming involved in his world of fantasy and then, unknowingly, he steps back into the reality of life situations. Thus the child is allowed to experience emotional growth under the most favorable conditions. As the child becomes emotionally relaxed during play, he can then experiment with his pent-up feelings. The counselor helps the child acknowledge the strong feelings expressed in his play as the disturbing conditions in his life. Then the child is able to examine those feelings and choose to accept or deny them as his own.

In play therapy the child is a doer, not a talker or observer. He expresses himself through what he chooses to do in play activity. In the play situation there is no lax time; every moment counts. The child is continually challenged by his imagination to demonstrate how he feels.

The counselor is present in play therapy to support the child as he reaches for emotional security. The counselor's role requires alertness, sensitivity, and an appreciation for what the child is doing and saying. It calls for great understanding and a genuine interest in the child. Axline (1969) has offered eight basic principles which influence the play therapist's role:

1. The therapist must develop a warm, friendly relationship with the child, in which good rapport is established as soon as possible.
2. The therapist accepts the child exactly as he is.
3. The therapist establishes a feeling permissiveness in the relationship so that the child is free to express his feelings completely.

4. The therapist is alert to recognize the *feelings* the child is expressing and reflects those feelings back to him in such a manner that he gains insight into his behavior.
5. The therapist maintains a deep respect for the child's ability to solve his own problems if given an opportunity to do so. The responsibility to make choices and to institute change is the child's.
6. The therapist does not attempt to direct the child's actions or conversation in any manner. The child leads the way; the therapist follows.
7. The therapist does not attempt to hurry the therapy along; it is a gradual process and is recognized as such by the therapist.
8. The therapist establishes only those limitations that are necessary to anchor the therapy to the world of reality and to make the child aware of his responsibility in the relationship.

The relationship established between the therapist and the child is the deciding factor in the success or failure of play therapy. Often it is not an easy relationship to establish.

An emotionally confused child is usually suspicious and bewildered by the new permissiveness of play therapy. Charles was no exception. During his second play session Charles was challenged to express his emotions by his counselor. She opened the door to the playroom and said:

> *Well, Charles, here we are again. You and me, just like I promised. Would you like to play with your doll again? Or would you like to do something different today?*

Charles responded by walking to the far corner of the room and picking up a small broken stick. He walked over to the sandbox and squatted next to it. He pulled the stick back and forth in the sand. Back and forth. Back and forth. His eyes followed the small grooves the stick made in the sand. Suddenly, Charles jumped up and threw the stick against the wall. He began to run around the room knocking toys off the shelves. He kicked any toys that fell in his way. After several minutes of his aggressive acting out, Charles stopped long enough to see what effect his behavior was having on the counselor. But she just watched and said nothing. She sensed that he was disappointed because she didn't yell at him to control his behavior.

When Charles tired of his wild playing, he went back to the sandbox and sat down. He reached over and pulled an adult male doll from the wreckage he had made and placed it face down in the sand. Slowly he began to bury the doll by pouring sand on it from his upraised hand. His face suggested strong concentration, but he didn't say a word. Soon the silence in the room became threatening. Finally, he asked the counselor, "Time to quit yet?"

The counselor said that ten minutes were left. Charles picked up the same black doll as before and crossed the room to stand beside his counselor. He held the doll out to her and said, "Looks like me, huh. . . ?" She responded, "Would you like the doll to look like you?" Charles shook his head and said, "He's better than me. He's got a mother and father. I ain't." The session ended when Charles squinted against the tears forming in his eyes and ran out of the room, saying, "Time to quit."

Charles was scheduled for morning and afternoon sessions for the next few days. He came back for his third play session the next afternoon. He entered the playroom with determination. "I wanta' do painting," he announced. He sat down at the small table and began to play with water paints. Yellow. Orange. Red. Black. He stirred the gooey red paint with his fingers. Charles began to spread the red paint in large streaks across his paper. He added a black border around the edge. The shades varied from deep red to lighter red and from black to grey. A small brown stick figure was added to the lower left edge. When he finished, Charles twisted his hand into a clawlike position and scratched his fingernails across the bottom of his wet painting. "There," he said. "It's done."

His counselor asked, "Would you like to tell me about it?" Charles explained slowly:

> *Things are burning all over. Fires all over . . . and lots of blood, man. They're all gettin' killed. Even my mean mom and dad and those other kids. This guy in the corner is safe. He's just watching all that blood. He musta' started the fires. He killed everybody. . . .*

The repetition of violent themes was a necessary part of play therapy for Charles. He was mirroring his view of the world he lived in.

A significant change occurred in Charles's behavior in the sixth play therapy session. It was Thursday afternoon. Charles entered the room and once again began to explore the water paints. Yellow. Red. Then brown. He slowly mixed the gooey brown paint in a small saucer. Suddenly he threw the paint saucer against the wall. The paint splattered into a heavy pattern and began to streak downward. Brown rivulets flowed down. The saucer clattered on the floor and then stopped. Nothing was said. Charles's face showed a large grin. He searched the counselor's eyes for a sign of disapproval or censure. The counselor watched Charles and said nothing. It was his move.

Suddenly Charles pounced at her. He ran at her with his brown fingers spread into clawlike weapons and his teeth bared. His face was twisted into a hideous mask and his eyes were wide with rage. "AAAGHHH," he screamed. Charles stopped short of her chair with his hands above his head, ready to strike. He stood there and searched his counselor's eyes for a clue to tell him how to behave. The counselor watched and waited, saying nothing. Slowly, Charles let his hands fall to his side. The look of terror and rage drained from his face. He began to cry. The counselor encouraged him to put his head in her lap. She began to stroke his neck and gave him the warmth of a person who cared. When the counselor told Charles that their hour together was almost gone, he raised his head and opened his tear-stained eyes. "You gonna let me come back here?" he asked. "Yes. Tomorrow morning."

The counselor recognized Charles's anger and fury as a positive expression of his fears. It was an encouraging sign; he felt safe enough in the playroom to express the fear and hostility growing inside of him. Though Charles could not understand his own behavior, his counselor understood the emotional struggle taking place. His display of anger toward her represented a constructive way to strike out symbolically at the adults who had been unfair to him. She felt that if Charles would continue to bring out his hostility in the playroom, he would soon move away from substitute targets.

Charles began the ninth play therapy session by standing on his tiptoes to look out the window. He looked across the rooftops of his old neighborhood and pointed out where he stayed with his grandmother. He could also see the bridge where he had tried to take his life. Charles said:

> You know, I don't never want to go back. They don't want me. I get in the way. I uhh . . . I get some crazy ideas sometimes. Like I could kill 'em all, sometimes. You understand. . . ?

He turned from the window to face his counselor. His verbal fantasy had allowed something to surface in his mind; his eyes were wide with excitement. Charles crossed the room and picked up several dolls. He arranged a mother doll, a father doll, and two small girl dolls along the edge of the sandbox. He appeared to be setting the stage for an important scene.

Charles didn't say anything. He stepped back from the row of dolls to look at them. Still he said nothing. The silence in the room hung heavily. Then, in a quick movement, Charles attacked the dolls. He doubled his fists and began beating on them. He killed the father doll first by pulling his head off. Then he stomped on a girl doll and pulled out a handful of her hair. Broken arms and legs flew everywhere. His teeth were clenched as tight as his fists. As he singled out the mother doll and began to beat it in the face, his eyes became cruel slits. "Bitch!" he cried. "Dirty old bitch! You never wanted me!" Charles grabbed a plastic fork from the debris and viciously stabbed the small mother doll. Charles stooped to stab the doll again and again. "There," he finally said, "I really messed 'em good." His clenched fists loosened but did not open. The battle within himself was done. A heavy sigh escaped from his chest.

Charles had consciously faced his wish to hurt his parents. It was clear that he wanted to retaliate against the feelings of guilt and worthlessness they gave him. Through making his parents smaller, Charles had been able to make himself bigger. Big enough not to be afraid to express his feelings toward them. He had gained enough courage in the playroom to look at his feelings for what they meant. This was an important breakthrough. If Charles couldn't recognize his anger, he would never learn how to control it. If he could learn to recognize his anger and the conditions that produced it, then he would be able to steer it into less destructive paths. He would control the expression of his anger instead of its controlling him.

As the counselor reflected on Charles's emotional growth in the playroom, she asked herself: Would he be able to cope with the fear that these thoughts and feelings had for him? Would he find the additional courage to go on? Charles gave her his answer the next morning. He didn't come to school. The next day a scribbled note from his grandmother indicated that Charles had run away.

OUTCOME

A recent phone call to Charles's mother proved to be unsatisfactory; she refused to have anything more to do with his disruptive behavior. Disclaiming any responsibility for his problems, she said:

*I just don't want no more to do with that boy. I got my own
family now and that's it. He's always been more trouble to me
than he's worth. He won't leave my two girls alone. Never gives
me a minute's peace. He's going to wind up in jail anyway, because that's where he wants to go. Lord knows Momma and I
tried. You understand. He's just never been any good. I don't
want no more to do with him and that's it. You understand?
Now I don't want you calling me no more. You understand. . . ?*

After repeated attempts to get Charles's grandmother to come to
the school failed, the counselor made a home visit. His grandmother
confronted the counselor on the porch and gruffly said that she hadn't
seen Charles for three days. She advised the counselor to "stop med-
dlin' in family things and let Charles be." She said, "You been stirrin'
him up at that school and it's no good. Just let him be. He'll come
home. He ain't got no place else to go."

The counselor is presently working with the community social
worker on legal procedures to make Charles a ward of the local court so
that placement can be made in a foster home or the church children's
center. As she reviewed her attempts to help Charles overcome his emotional problems, the counselor said:

*From the beginning, I knew I couldn't change the awful stuff
he had to live with. But at least I tried to give him some tools to
help him understand what was going on. Charles was desperate
to find someone or someplace to belong to. In the play therapy
room, he was learning that he wasn't all bad; he wanted to be
loved for himself, like all children. He knew some good things
were deep down inside of him. His play sessions gave him a small
release for his feelings and opened a door that could have led to
self-understanding. But Charles didn't make it through that door.*

FOCUS QUESTIONS

1. Each of us views the world through the prism of our own preju-
   dices. In play therapy the child is encouraged to move from the
   hidden and indirect feelings of anxiety and hostility toward open
   expression of his feelings. How would you have encouraged Charles
   to generalize his successful play experiences to the world he lived in?

41

2. Good relations between the school counselor and the teachers she works with are an essential part of play therapy. Assume that you are a new counselor in an elementary school that does not have a play therapy program. Can you identify three things you would do to create staff support for such a program?

3. A child is usually quick to accept life as he finds it; he will find a way to adapt to his home environment and the people he lives with. Unfortunately, Charles couldn't. If you were the counselor in this case, what recommendations would you make to: the school administration, the family, or Charles's teachers?

4. Through play therapy, Charles was offered a human relationship which carried some hope of growth and change for him. How would you rate the effectiveness of the counseling process described in this case?

5. A child takes little and big things from the world around him and weaves fantasies about his life. How can adults, who have come to believe only in logic, reach out to understand the confused thoughts of children?

BIBLIOGRAPHY: CHARLES

Ginott, Haim G. *Group Psychotherapy With Children.* New York: McGraw-Hill Book Co., 1961.

Axline, Virginia M. *Play Therapy.* New York: Ballantine Books, 1969.

CRITIQUE OF THE CASE OF CHARLES

Charles, the counselee in this case study, was between eleven and twelve years old. Yet his treatment was play therapy, where doll play was the basic medium used, in addition to counselor-counselee talk. As a pre-adolescent, Charles was beyond the doll play stage and therefore a more appropriate form of treatment would likely have been activity therapy. Because preadolescents are physically, intellectually, and emotionally beyond the doll playing stage, involvement in games and gamelike activities is usually the preferred mode of treatment. In the case of Charles, some physical or recreational activity such as shooting baskets, playing catch, playing table tennis, checkers, billiards, and similar activities with the counselor would have been more appropriate to his developmental level (Gazda, 1971).

Ideally, too, Charles's counselor might better have been a black male with whom Charles could identify and model. Rather than encouraging Charles to regress to a stage of infantilism through playing with dolls that could be demeaning, a more positive approach might first involve helping Charles change his image by building up his masculinity through a physical fitness program. He could develop his physical prowess and his image as a man while releasing his pent-up energy. His intellectual skills were limited because he was too anxious and depressed to concentrate on subject matter material. Involvement in a physical skill development area would require less intellectual concentration yet allow the counselor to be actively involved with Charles through the exercises or games themselves.

Preadolescents find it quite difficult to self-disclose with adults. Yet when they can relate to adults, usually of the same sex, through activities, they can drop their defenses, and many spontaneous disclosures occur because their anxiety level is reduced. After a good relationship had been developed with Charles, activity and/or concurrent activity-interview group counseling would be a treatment of choice, as a method to improve his social and interpersonal interactions with his peer group.

Since Charles was very depressed at times, it would seem that he might have benefited also from some chemotherapy while receiving activity or activity-interview therapy. But more important than any of the interventions suggested to this point, Charles was living under intolerable conditions, and to expect him to improve or change while so trapped is to expect too much. His maladaptive behavior appeared to be precipitated as a means of escaping his home environment; to treat him without changing the basic source of his trouble would be to get him to adjust to an intolerable situation.

The most useful counselor intervention, therefore, would have been to take immediate steps to remove Charles from his home environment and then provide individual activity and activity-interview group counseling. Of course, legal steps would be required in removing Charles from his home. Nevertheless, little change could be expected from Charles when most of the external events impinging on him were unchanged. As the case itself demonstrated, this was eventually a necessary action.

Discussion Questions

1. A suggested preferred intervention in the case of Charles is to take immediate steps to have Charles removed from his home environment. Cite reasons which support this recommendation and reasons which do not support it.
2. Consider the counselor skills needed to begin legal action to have Charles removed from his home environment. Do you possess these skills? If not, should counselors be trained in these skills? If you do not possess this type of intervention skill, to whom would you turn when such an intervention is required?
3. Be prepared to defend the use of play therapy with Charles as described in the actual treatment.
4. Be prepared to defend the use of a combination of individual activity and group activity-interview counseling as suggested in the Critique of the Case of Charles.

Bibliography: Critique of Charles

Gazda, George M. *Group Counseling: A Developmental Approach.* Boston: Allyn and Bacon, 1971.

II

Adolescents

Sherri

At 7 A.M., with carefully practiced movements, Sherri entered the family bathroom to draw a glass of water. After "popping" two downers (depressant barbiturates) and drinking the water, Sherri returned to her room to finish dressing and prepare for school. Then, locking her room behind her, she called goodbye to her parents and sister who were still finishing breakfast and left to join her friends outside the nearby junior high school. At thirteen years of age, still in the eighth grade, Sherri had entered the drug scene which has spread in epidemic proportions among school children.

Later that same morning, Sherri took her first half-tab of "Strawberry Acid" (pink LSD) during her math class "to cool it and black out the world around me." Because she was inexperienced with the drug and did not feel its effects after fifteen minutes, Sherri dropped a second half-tab of "Strawberry" supplied by her boyfriend. When the bell rang to end class, Sherri began a psychological trip that was unlike any experience she had ever known before. As she left class and entered the hallway, she was startled and frightened by the hustle-bustle noises of class change. She crouched in terror in a hallway corner to hide from the threatening roar of slamming lockers and ringing bells. In her drug-heightened state of awareness, Sherri could see streaks of bright lights encircling students walking in the hallway. When a close friend approached to ask why she wasn't going to her next class, Sherri responded by physically attacking her and screaming, "You'll never kill me! I'll get you first! You'll *never* get me!"

Then, in a brief moment Sherri's behavior completely changed; she slumped to the floor and quietly stared downward, repeating the phrase, "Good girl . . . I'm a good girl." Her bewildered friend, Pam, hurriedly sought out the principal for help; together they managed to walk Sherri slowly down to the counselor's office and placed her in a sitting position on the floor. Sherri said that she could see "traces of light" behind the body of movements of people around her and asked Pam to stay close to her because she was really scared. Pam told the principal that she had been around friends on drugs before and volunteered to try to "talk Sherri down from her trip." The principal agreed and quickly made attempts to locate the counselor who was, ironically, attending an in-service training session dealing with drug abuse in the school. The counselor was introduced to the situation by the principal's comment over the phone: "You've got a crisis sitting on your office floor. Please come back to the school immediately!"

BACKGROUND

To outward appearances, Sherri comes from a pleasant middle-class home. Her parents live in a comfortable brick four-bedroom ranch-style home in a new suburban housing development adjacent to a large city. Her parents have been married sixteen years and attend the Catholic church regularly. They have three daughters: Judy, age fifteen, Sherri, age thirteen, and Debbie, age ten. Her father completed high school and owns a small appliance repair shop which employs three men. Her mother is a high school graduate but has no work experience other than her role as housewife; she seldom leaves the home except for important social functions.

A more careful appraisal of Sherri's home environment reveals a great deal of psychological tension and frequent emotional outbursts between the mother and her daughters. Both of Sherri's parents had been married and divorced prior to their present marriage, and this serves as a constant source of friction between her parents. Each partner often accuses the other of infidelity before the children. A compounding factor related to the hostility between Sherri's parents is the large amount of alcohol consumed by her mother each evening.

Sherri had her first counselor contact when she and her mother came to the school to enroll Sherri for the seventh grade. Sherri appeared to the counselor to be a friendly and energetic youth, eager to learn. Her grade school records indicated that Sherri had been an outstanding student in all of her academic subjects and was well liked by her classmates. She had participated in many extracurricular activities and had been elected as a seventh grade cheerleader. Sherri's family moved during the summer after she had completed sixth grade in a parochial school. During the orientation conference, Sherri expressed a desire to make new friends quickly and demonstrated anguish about the missed cheerleading opportunity. Her mother was somewhat concerned about possible academic problems related to the different teaching methods used in public and parochial school systems.

Sherri did not visit her counselor again until the second semester of the school year. The counselor immediately noticed that Sherri's personal vitality and easygoing outward appearance were gone. Her ready smile and quick humor had been replaced by hesitant glances and incomplete sentences. She had scheduled the visit with her counselor to clarify a grade change in her math class, but quickly turned the conversation toward her personal problems at home. After gaining a promise from her counselor that her information would be kept in strict confidentiality, Sherri began to talk about what had happened at her home the previous night.

Judy, Sherri's older sister, had come home from visiting at a friend's house at the appointed curfew hour of nine o'clock. However, Sherri's mother challenged Judy by saying that she had arrived ten minutes late. In the tense series of heated remarks that followed, Judy called her mother a "drunken hag" and said she was going to move out as soon as possible. Her mother countered by accusing Judy of becoming a "neighborhood slut" and slapped her face. An ugly physical brawl began between mother and daughter. It ended when Judy was hit with a heavy broken lamp that caused a large bloody wound on her arm. Sherri's father, who had been a spectator during the fight, separated the two women and then took Judy to the hospital for medical treatment.

When Judy and her father returned home they found Sherri's mother in the front lawn in a very drunken condition. She shouted obscene names at Judy and said that she was going to put her in a nearby home for unmanageable girls in the morning. Sherri's father said very little to his wife and managed to return Judy to her bedroom and asked her to lock the door. Sherri spent the rest of the night helping to clean up the house and listening to her mother cursing the day she had given birth to Judy. Early the next morning, before Sherri and Debbie left for school, her mother and father took Judy in the family car to commit her to the private Home For Juvenile Girls.

As Sherri talked about these experiences with her counselor, she began to cry. She said that she was worried about Judy and what would happen to her at that "home." She was also very worried about how to protect Debbie and herself from physical beatings when her mother had been drinking. Sherri said that she loved her father but she didn't think he would stand up to her mother "when the going gets tough." As Sherri got ready to leave for her next class, she said:

> Well, thanks. At least you listened to me and tried to help. Most adults don't understand. They don't listen. . . . Sometimes I talk about it to the other kids. Lots of 'em are in the same boat, you know. And . . . well, they understand me, but they can't help. You're different. I like adults who understand and listen. Too many are like my grandmother; if you tell her something, she gives you a lecture. Well, see you later.

As Sherri was leaving her office, the counselor encouraged her to come back the next day for another visit. Sherri promised to come back if she was having trouble. It was a promise Sherri didn't keep.

INITIAL COUNSELING INTERVIEW

After receiving the phone call from the principal at her school, the counselor immediately returned to her office to learn more about the "crisis sitting on her floor."

As she entered her office, she recognized Sherri slumped on the floor with her arms folded around her knees. Sherri was talking to Pam about how the furniture in the office was "slanting toward her and moving around." As the counselor quietly closed the door, Sherri shouted that the door was going to hit her in the face and struggled to protect herself from the impact she imagined. Shortly afterward, she sat upright and began to slowly move a pencil back and forth horizontally in front of her red and dilated eyes. She wanted to watch the "traces of light the pencil left behind." For the next twenty minutes Sherri alternately laughed and cried at the beauty of "traces" and "vibrations" coming from Pam and the counselor. The tension and anxiety in the room reached a crescendo as Sherri began to writhe on the floor and sob hysterically; she cried out that her left leg was gone and she could feel fuzzy things crawling all over her body.

Fortunately, the counselor's previous training enabled her to control the natural urge to touch and comfort Sherri. She knew that people in a drug-heightened state of awareness are easily provoked to physical attack because they are unreasonably frightened by someone touching them or moving around near to them. The counselor responded to Sherri by slowly sitting down on the floor near to her and talking in a controlled voice, saying, "Sherri, everything is going to be all right now. I won't let any furniture fall on you and I'll make the fuzzy things go away." This response had a remarkable effect on Sherri. She sensed the counselor's efforts to help her return from her acid trip and her behavior became more rational.

Four hours after Sherri's trip began, she was psychologically and physically exhausted. In her conversation with her counselor, she began to respond normally to her counselor's questions with the calm relief of her spent emotions. Sherri explained that her trip was prompted by a particularly ugly scene that morning before school. Her mother had found some cigarettes in Sherri's coat pocket and accused her of being a thief. She showered Sherri with comments like: "I don't know why I ever had you. You were just a big mistake." Sherri began crying and pleaded with her mother to "just leave me alone." Her mother countered by slapping Sherri's face and said, "Stop sassing me or I'll put you in the car and take you to the girls' home, like we did Judy!"

Sherri said that she decided that morning before school that she just couldn't take it anymore. Her mother was drinking more than ever and had hit her several times. Sherri wept as she explained that she had been trying harder than ever to be good at home during the past two weeks. But it didn't do any good. Her mother always found something wrong with her. She said she couldn't stand having to cook dinner for the whole family and then have her mother say something like: "Is dinner ready yet, you little bitch?"

When Sherri turned to her father to gain help and understanding, he developed a peculiar behavior pattern; each evening when he came home from work he ate his dinner in fifteen minutes and then went to bed with the understanding he was not to be "bothered by anyone" until it was time to go to work in the morning. Sherri summed up her feelings about her home situation with the blunt comment: "I want out."

Sherri felt that she could strike back at her mother by taking drugs in school and calling home to say, "I'm freaked out on acid, Mom, because you pushed me too far. You and your drinking and swearing. What do you think of me now?"

Sherri explained to her counselor that she had been so nervous and agitated before swallowing the drugs, she didn't care what happened to her body because she wanted to become calm and dreamy like her boyfriend promised she would. After her bad trip on acid was over, Sherri said her immediate fears were about flashback grips and getting busted for using drugs in school. She definitely did not want to go home. Her counselor contacted the community social worker who had worked with Judy's case and explained Sherri's dilemma. The social worker agreed that Sherri should not go home and suggested that she be placed in the Juvenile Services Shelter Home for a few days. Sherri thought it was a good solution.

Twenty minutes later an officer from the Juvenile Shelter arrived at the school to take Sherri to the County Mental Health Center for a complete physical examination prior to placement. Before Sherri left the counselor's office, she asked the counselor if she would be willing to visit her the next day. Her counselor quickly agreed.

The next problem that faced the counselor was that of notifying Sherri's mother about what had happened at school. The counselor called Sherri's mother and related the events that had happened. Her mother responded that she knew Sherri had been running around with a bad crowd at school and that she knew she couldn't trust Sherri anymore. Her mother indicated that Sherri was no longer welcome at home; if she returned, her mother would place her in custody of the Home For Juvenile Girls where Judy was.

Another important problem the counselor had to deal with was the role of the principal in this case. Confidentiality of information related to Sherri's case was made difficult because it was the principal himself who walked Sherri to the counselor's office with her friend Pam. Fortunately, the principal had created an excellent working relationship with his counselor. He said that he had faith in the counselor's judgment and asked only to be kept informed of the important aspects of Sherri's progress. He stated that Sherri must be automatically suspended from the school for three weeks or until evidence of rehabilitation was demonstrated. He suggested that perhaps a long-term solution to her problems might be to place her in a foster home. Hopefully, Sherri would find some caring adults who could help her find value in herself. He concluded:

*We have to suspend Sherri . . . no way to get around that.
But I'm not sure that enforcement of our rules is the answer. It's
the kids like her who need help. We can't help them if they
aren't here. You know, we're so enforcement oriented, I don't
know what I would do if a student came in to ask for help to
drop his habit. Maybe send him to the counselor. . . .*

The counselor visited Sherri at the Juvenile Shelter the next morning and witnessed a dramatic change in her behavior. Sherri exhibited a
great deal of personal composure and smiled frequently at her counselor as she discussed her feelings about her trip. She said that she felt
glad to be rid of the pressure that had been "bottled and twisted up
inside." Sherri summed it up in her comment: "I feel like a new me."
Her counselor considered her buoyant mood possibly to be a result of
the sudden and immediate tension release afforded by the drug experience. At the end of the interview, the counselor asked Sherri if she
would participate in daily hour-long counseling sessions with her for
two weeks. Sherri quickly agreed. The counselor left as arrangements
were being made for a Juvenile Parole Officer to accompany Sherri to
her home to pick up her clothing and personal things.

COUNSELING METHODOLOGY

Sherri's counselor chose client-centered counseling methods for several
important reasons: (1) Sherri was intelligent and could express herself
clearly, (2) modification of behavior in the home environment was
unlikely, and (3) Sherri and her counselor found it easy to relate to
each other. Client-centered or nondirective counseling methods have
been developed primarily from the writings of Carl Rogers (1951). This
form of counseling places great importance on the subjective relationship developed between the counselor and his client during the counseling process. A fundamental characteristic of client-centered counseling
is the strong emotional bond created between counselor and client.

Shertzer and Stone (1968) have suggested that the basic constructs
of "self" and the "experienced world" provide a helpful understanding
of the theory supporting client-centered methods. The self develops
through the person's interactions with his environment, and these interactions are in turn influenced by the developing self. Each person per-

53

ceives his world in accordance with his developing self-concept, so that his interactions with his environment become highly personalized. His experienced world of reality becomes colored by his concept of himself. He behaves in a manner consistent with his developing self-concept. The person becomes an individual by defining himself to others through his behavior in interpersonal situations. He will reinforce or modify his self-concept through his perception of the impact of his behavior on others.

A person with a healthy personality has a self-concept that is reasonably consistent or congruent with reality. The individual can perceive his environment adequately and understand his personal experiences. He remains in close touch with reality and can easily incorporate new behaviors to meet demands of the external world. If the individual's self-concept is incongruent with reality, he is likely to have personal problems.

Incongruence of personality and behavior occurs when a person attempts to project an unrealistic or false self-concept. He distorts the reality of the external world by denying an aspect of himself that he does not want to accept or share with others. His distortion of reality and the denial of part of his behavior can create two unfortunate situations: (1) the continual effort to deny a negative part of personal behavior causes anxiety, and (2) the distortion of true circumstances makes it difficult for the person to deal directly with the cause of his anxiety. The result is a person who is anxious and unhappy, but does not understand why; he cannot acknowledge the feelings which are causing his unhappiness.

Client-centered counseling is based on the assumption that each person has a potential for growth and self-actualization; every individual possesses a natural drive to become a worthwhile, unique person. The positive self-concept of the individual will emerge when he can allow himself to experience his true feelings openly and honestly. He must be free to look at his good and bad characteristics and to accept himself as he really is. The counseling process is designed to provide a nonthreatening atmosphere in which the person can lower his defenses and explore his own capabilities.

A counselor using client-centered methods communicates three important attitudes to his client: (1) positive regard, (2) empathic understanding, and (3) congruence. Positive regard is created when the counselor cares about his client. The caring should be nonpossessive, nonevaluative, and without reservations; the counselor must project genuine concern and positive feelings toward his client. He should not impose his value system on his client or make the reservation that he may withdraw his positive regard if he finds the client's past behavior offensive. Empathic understanding is an accurate moment-to-moment awareness of his client's present feelings toward his behavior. Congruence means that the counselor must be himself; he must not role-play at understanding. He should be genuine and actually feel some of the emotional turmoil of his client. For client-centered counseling to be successful, these attitudes must be communicated by the counselor and understood by his client.

The techniques of nondirective counseling are deceptively simple. The role of the counselor is to listen carefully to what the client is trying to communicate. The counselor attempts to understand the internal frame of reference of his client by thinking, feeling, and exploring things related to his personal problems. During the counseling session the counselor often says things designed to clarify or reflect emotional content. This effort expresses respect and understanding for feelings shared by his client. The counselor's behavior is directed toward facilitating his client's ability to consciously recognize and understand feelings associated with previous behavior.

The initial requirement for the counselor in client-centered counseling is to accept his client as a worthwhile, unique human being. Sherri and her counselor felt the mutual respect and trust necessary to form a client-centered counseling relationship.

Sherri and her counselor began the third counseling session while sitting on opposite ends of a bunk bed in her room at the Shelter. Her counselor first asked Sherri, "How are you today?" Sherri responded by saying that she was glad to see her counselor because some things were "heavy on her mind." The first thing she talked about was her visit home to pick up her clothes and personal belongings. She said:

> It was awful. Soon as I went in the door I cried like everything. Somehow I just didn't want to leave there. . . . Mom was gone so that made it easier. But I felt so empty inside, like I was leaving everything behind me.

The second thing that Sherri talked about was her lack of interest in school. She confessed that she hadn't done any homework for two weeks and didn't feel like doing any. Thinking about her problems took most of her attention. Sherri described herself as being physically tired all the time and yet simultaneously tense and uptight. She explained that her "stomach felt like it was always tied in small knots," especially when she and her mother were arguing at home. Sherri said that she was always seeking a relaxed feeling of calm inner peace that she used to get when she was having a good time with her friends at her old school.

After talking about her physical and psychological problems for a few more minutes, Sherri stopped and quietly stared downward at her shoes. After a long significant pause, she blurted out, "Can speed really alter your chromosomes?" Her counselor, surprised by the question, understood that Sherri was not asking for a philosophical maybe answer. She wanted to know factual data. She was looking for an answer that would have a direct impact on her life. The counselor gave Sherri an honest and straightforward answer:

> *I don't know if it can or not, nobody knows for sure. The research is still not complete. But I do know that if somebody turns to drugs to escape personal problems, the problems are still there when they come down from the drugs.*

Sherri thought about what her counselor had said for a while and then revealed that her question was a result of a discussion that she and some other girls had held that morning. She knew some of her friends at school were using soft drugs (stimulants for "ups" and depressants for "downers") frequently, and they were eager to experiment with grass and acid to take a trip. Sherri said that she was worried about her friends because, "you wouldn't believe how ignorant those kids are about the stuff they swallow."

The remainder of the third counseling session focused on the use of drugs in the school. Sherri claimed that there were only a few "druggies" at the school presently, but they were hustling others to experiment with them. She concluded:

> *Most of the kids are like me. Not really bad homes or anything, but a lot of tension. Not the generation gap thing, either. Just a feeling that they ought to try everything once. Believe me, I never thought I'd be an acid eater.*

Sherri and her counselor began the fourth counseling session while sitting crosslegged on the floor in her room at the Shelter. The counselor asked Sherri some open-ended questions designed to explore the development of her feelings toward drugs. Sherri easily responded:

56

*All my girl friends talked about boys and liquor. I didn't
understand it at all. Then one time I was at my friend's house
and she offered me some beer. Just like that. I said I didn't want
it, but she said I was chicken. That's just what you don't want to
hear, so I drank it. Then we drank some wine and I got high.
Boy, did I ever get high!*

*Pretty soon the floor seemed a lot wider and the ceiling
began to spin. Everything looked different, you know. It was
funny. We both laughed and laughed. Then I got dizzy and threw
up. All over her good bedspread. It was awful. Then I got scared.
I thought, how can I drink like this when I hated my mother for
drinking so much? That was it for me.*

Another important topic that Sherri seemed eager to talk about was
her feelings of uneasiness around most adults. Sherri explained:

*I don't know what it is. I just get this feeling like they resent
me somehow. I think that adults really don't understand how
kids feel about things. Like me. I've been doing drugs, right.
Well, adults will just say, "Why didn't you think about what
would happen?" Well, I don't know. I guess you just don't think
about it. I wish they could just read our minds and understand.
Most parents and the teachers are a lot alike. They are all just a
bunch of answers. . . . They always make you feel dumber than
you are.*

After Sherri had been in the Juvenile Services Shelter Home for
three days, a juvenile hearing was held at the county courthouse to
decide her legal future. Her parents appeared at the hearing and requested that Sherri be placed in the Home For Juvenile Girls because
she was a "juvenile delinquent" who directly disobeyed her parents.
When the judge asked Sherri's mother to describe her daughter's behavior, she said, "I can't trust her anymore, and I would rather she be put
somewhere where they lock her up at night than running the streets
with her friends, using drugs. She's as bad as her sister, and I won't put
up with them anymore." Sherri's father passively watched the floor and
said nothing.

During the hearing the counselor was granted permission to talk to
the judge as a friend of the court in the privacy of the judge's chambers.
With Sherri's permission, the counselor gave the judge information
related to her physical and psychological punishment at home. The

school principal and community social worker also testified during the hearing and were united in their recommendation that Sherri be placed in a foster home. The judge found Sherri to be "in need of supervision" and legally made her a ward of the court, pending placement in an adequate foster home.

The sixth counseling session took place in the counselor's office at school. Sherri was granted permission to visit her counselor at school for one hour. The session began when Sherri announced that she thought that it would be the last counseling session. She said:

> *I like you and all that, Mrs. ____, but I'm really confused about how you can help me much anymore. We talk about things, you know, about me . . . and I dump my problems out. I, umm, I guess I feel a little better. But, uhh, but I know when I leave here and walk out the door, you know, all my problems are still there. Nothing's changed or anything and that's a real downer. . . .*

Her counselor responded:

> *Sherri, I can accept that. But let's explore how you feel about it. My guess is that you feel lonely and cut-off right now. Sort of separated from everything that was important to you— your friends and family. Is that how you feel?*

Sherri answered that her counselor was right. She was feeling very depressed and unwanted. Her fears about finding a place to live in a foster home were growing. The counselor tried to give Sherri feelings of support when she said:

> *Sherri, the most important thing to me is that you care about yourself. You are a special person to me and there's no-body else like you. Most of us worry about our problems a lot, but the problems we have tell us about who we are. I think you'll find the courage to face your problems. I'd like to help you.*

The remainder of the sixth session focused on Sherri's feelings of depression. She tentatively accepted her counselor's definition of depression: feelings of resentment and anger turned inward. Sherri said that she felt that perhaps her trip was actually a way of expressing her bad feelings toward her mother. Evidence that Sherri was beginning to

accept the responsibility for her own feelings and behavior surfaced
when she said:

> *My mother is a tough problem. Somehow she makes me feel
> guilty. Like I never tried hard or anything. Like I could never be
> worth anything. She makes me feel bad about her drinking and
> problems, but I've got problems of my own. I've got to figure
> out my own problems and get straight. My real problem is to
> decide what I want out of life. Maybe then the rest will sort of
> fall into place.*

Sherri agreed to keep her feelings "up front" where she could share
them honestly with others. When she asked for another counseling
session in a couple of days to explore her feelings about herself, the
counselor readily agreed.

The seventh counseling session took place three days later in
Sherri's room at the Shelter. Sherri called and asked the counselor to
visit her because she was feeling very low. Although many of her friends
and several teachers had visited her to renew their friendship and offer
encouragement, Sherri said she was confused and lonely. The counselor
asked Sherri to talk about how she felt about herself as a person. Sherri
offered a complex answer:

> *I'm a pretty face. A name. Somebody nice to be around. To
> my mother, I'm a child she doesn't want. To my teachers, I'm a
> problem and a challenge. A question mark. To you, I'm honest
> and we like each other. You know the rest of that.*
>
> *On the inside, I'm mixed up. Parts of different people at
> different times. Sometimes a teenager. But mostly adult. Even a
> little bit child, sometimes. It's like I'm pieces of some kind of
> puzzle that looks like it will never fit together. That hurts, you
> know. . . .*

The counselor let the silence fill the room before she replied:

> *Sherri, sometimes all of us get physically and emotionally
> run down and confused. We see ourselves only as victims of
> what's going on today . . . today's problems. We forget that we
> create our own tomorrows. Many of us don't want to meet the
> challenge of today, so we turn around and hang onto yesterday's
> problems. Sort of rehearsing them again in our minds. It isn't*

easy to trade our miserable feelings for something we don't
know much about. Does any of that make sense to you?

Sherri thought about what her counselor said and then answered:

I want to understand. It's like some poetry I read once. It
said we can all grow, not just physical growth, but in how we can
understand ourselves. And we can grow by being good to people
who need us, right?

Two days later, Sherri agreed to a "trial home visit" with a foster
family in her community. Two young girls lived in the new home:
Kathy who was Sherri's age and Laura who was two years younger.
Their father was employed as a postal clerk and spent a great deal of his
free time with his daughters working on family projects. Their mother
had been an elementary school teacher prior to becoming a housewife.
She enjoyed doing volunteer work with patients at the nearby mental
health clinic. Sherri was to live with her new "family" for two weeks; if
the placement was acceptable to everyone, the judge would then grant
temporary legal custody of Sherri to her foster parents.

OUTCOME

When Sherri moved into the foster home, she began attending a junior
high school located across town from where she had previously gone to
school. She quickly developed new friendships and her grades were
above average. One week after Sherri had transferred schools, her foster
parents visited her previous counselor to learn about Sherri's "danger
points." The foster parents explained that Sherri was desperately trying
to please them and to be a "good girl." They communicated a sincere
interest in Sherri's welfare and expressed a desire to do everything possible to help her become a happy young person.

Sherri is presently completing the eighth grade and has made an
excellent adjustment in her foster home. During the spring semester
break, Sherri returned to her counselor for a friendly visit. She began
by talking about how she felt about herself:

You know, I think I can make it the way I am. So many
things have happened to me since I saw you last. Good things,

you know. . . . But mostly, a chance to live in a real *home where people care about each other. My friend Kathy is really neat.*

Sherri explained that she and her foster mother had become very close. "She's a real woman. She gives you a chance to explain yourself and treats you fair." Sherri described her foster father as "a real nut," always ready to try anything.

Sherri's present problems seem to focus on developing her self-respect and a personal sense of worth. Her foster parents and their daughter Kathy have helped her to learn that she is a unique person. Sherri is now discovering that she is worthy of consideration and respect from her friends.

FOCUS QUESTIONS

1. Children learn their drug habits from their parents. "Mom takes pills to wake up, to calm her down, and even to not make babies. . . ." How can counselors help young people learn that there is no chemical cure for unpleasant life situations?
2. The counseling relationship between Sherri and her counselor was closer and more intense than ordinary social friendships. Identify three important characteristics of the counselor's attitude or behavior toward Sherri that enabled her to work effectively as a client-centered school counselor.
3. The behavior of Sherri's parents strongly influenced her attitude toward them as well as the development of her personality. Do you think her parents could have benefited from counseling services too? Would you suggest individual or group therapy? What mental health services (public and private) would be available to them in your community?
4. The world has experienced tremendous technological advances and scientific exploration while Sherri was growing up. The speedup in technology and communication seems to be linked to a short-coming of emotional adjustment among young people. Can counselors teach young people how to cope with an ever-changing world?
5. The principal-counselor working relationship described in this case was characterized by mutual respect and understanding. Would you predict a different counseling outcome for drug abuse students if that kind of relationship did not exist?

BIBLIOGRAPHY: SHERRI

Rogers, Carl R. *Client-Centered Therapy*. Boston: Houghton Mifflin, 1951.

Shertzer, Bruce, and Stone, Shelley. *Fundamentals of Counseling.* Boston: Houghton Mifflin, 1968.

CRITIQUE OF THE CASE OF SHERRI

The counselor in the case of Sherri was described as client-centered; however, she seemed to be quite flexible and willing to act in an evaluative manner when necessary. For example, she contacted the social worker and prevented Sherri from having to return to a home that was responsible for her desperate condition. The willingness of the counselor to involve all those who could help Sherri and also her willingness to meet with Sherri daily following her leaving school was commendable. This contact was certainly important in Sherri's learning to trust an adult, which she desperately needed. The counselor's willingness to intercede with the judge on behalf of Sherri to have her placed in a foster home rather than a detention home was also laudatory. The fact that she obtained Sherri's permission before she shared Sherri's home condition with the judge was an example of good ethical conduct and respect for the counselee.

There were a few instances in the case of Sherri where the counselor was not following good counseling procedures. First, following her first counseling contact with Sherri before the acid trip, the counselor should have been able to recognize the potential problems of Sherri and instead of "encouraging Sherri to come back the next day for a visit," the counselor should have made a specific appointment with Sherri; then perhaps she would have returned, and the counselor could have prevented the drug scene which occurred later.

A second questionable counselor response was her answer to Sherri's question: "Can speed really alter your chromosomes?" The counselor gave an honest answer of "I don't know . . . nobody knows for sure," but then turned her response into a mini lecture with: "But I do know that if somebody turns to drugs to escape personal problems, the problems are still there when they come down from the drugs." This response was disrespectful because obviously Sherri also knew that much.

A third questionable counselor response occurred during the seventh session. Sherri was trying to put the pieces of her problem together, and the counselor responded to Sherri in the third person rather than directly. She also universalized her response rather than focusing directly on Sherri.

During the sixth counseling session Sherri seemed ready to terminate counseling prematurely because she couldn't see how the counselor was helping her solve her problems. Chances are that the counselor had been too nondirective in the first five interviews, i.e., the counselor had not been able to move the counselee into depth exploration and action. In other words, she may have lacked action intervention skills *à la* Carkhuff. This condition is somewhat substantiated in that the counselor had made no effort to get Sherri to formulate specific goals to work on in the counseling relationship.

Although the counselor held seven interviews with Sherri and tried to help her understand herself, it seems that the counselor's willingness to intervene directly to remove Sherri from her home and the conditions contributing directly to her problems was the most helpful gesture that could have been made. The second most important effort on the part of the counselor was to gather support to have Sherri placed in an appropriate foster home. Under these new conditions Sherri made excellent progress because she was allowed to fulfill herself.

Discussion Questions

1. If you had been Sherri's school counselor, would you have taken the same steps in behalf of Sherri? If not, why not?
2. Do you think that the counselor's stated philosophy of being client-centered gave her any unique skills for working with Sherri beyond those possessed by a behaviorally oriented counselor? If so, what were they?
3. What situations in Sherri's case were dependent upon a team approach for the successful outcome?
4. Would you have handled the talking down of Sherri when she was on her trip differently than the counselor in this case? If so, what specifically would you have done differently?
5. Using the Carkhuff base building or facilitative phase and dimensions of empathy, respect, and warmth, simulate through role-playing a counseling session with Sherri during the first visit to her at the Shelter.

Bibliography: Critique of Sherri

Carkhuff, Robert R. *The Development of Human Resources.* New York: Holt, Rinehart and Winston, 1971.

Connie

Connie was confused and lonely. She came to the campus counseling center because there was no place else to go. She had spent the last several nights alone, in the darkened balcony of the Catholic church. When Father Anthony learned of Connie's solitary all-night vigils, he recommended that she visit the counseling center for psychological help.

When Connie came into his office, the counselor noticed her confused and unsettled appearance. She was wearing a too-big, weather-faded army fatigue jacket and large baggy jeans. Her long dark hair hadn't been combed for several days; it hung over her thin, angular face, and fell into her eyes when she looked down, which seemed to be a familiar posture to her. She came into the office and slumped into a large chair. Her first words were:

> *I don't know why I'm here. You see a lot of people who need help more than I do. But I'm really spooked. . . . I just don't know what is happening to me. I just think about death all the time. . . . Nothing has answers anymore and I'm really spooked. . . .*

These statements were followed by high-pitched, broken laughter that was to become characteristic of her early therapeutic sessions.

BACKGROUND

Connie was an eighteen-year-old freshman at a large southwestern university when she entered therapy at the campus counseling center. She lived in a large tower-like residence hall with 800 other women, sharing her room with two freshmen girls named Betsy and Martha. Connie's parents lived in an upper-middle-class suburban housing development located in a city with a population of 300,000. Her parents had two daughters and a son living at home: Mary, age twenty-two, Linda, age fifteen, and eight-year-old David.

Connie's father was employed as a distributor for a large paint manufacturing company. He traveled to many large retail customer locations throughout his three-state sales territory and frequently was gone from home. Though he quit school in the eleventh grade, rapid promotions and salary increases described her father's vocational success. On many occasions Connie's father encouraged her to go to college to "better herself and her family."

Connie didn't want to talk about her mother. Until she developed feelings of trust in her therapist, she thwarted his attempts to investigate this area by abruptly changing the subject. Eventually Connie explained that she was embarrassed to talk about her mother because she was a heavy drinker. Her mother drank three or more double martinis almost every night. Connie said her mother seemed to drink because she wanted to be affectionate toward her father, regain her sense of "womanliness," and feel sexy. After a few drinks, her mother became more loving toward her children and husband. Connie said that her mother was usually uptight, always talking in carefully measured sentences. She said her mother talks as if she is weighing each word in her own mind first, so she can predict the impact of what she says on the other person.

Connie's older sister Mary also had emotional problems. Mary had attended the same university where Connie was enrolled, but dropped out during her sophomore year because of pregnancy. Mary turned down the marriage offer by the father of her child. When her daughter was born, she put her up for adoption. Two months later she accepted her boyfriend's second marriage proposal. Mary's marriage lasted only three months. The husband sued for divorce because Mary returned to her mother on the slightest excuse. He had told Connie, "Your sister's got no identity of her own. I feel like I'm married to your mother." Soon after the divorce was final, Mary bought a small house near her parents' home so that she could visit her mother daily. Connie admitted that she had some feelings of resentment toward Mary because of the amount of attention her mother gave her. She countered those feelings by reasoning that she wanted her freedom and independence much more than the material things they could give her.

Connie demonstrated high academic ability as a student in high school. She graduated with honors from a school with an enrollment of 3,300 students. She had received high grades in many subjects but she was particularly gifted in political science. During her first semester at the university Connie enrolled in several honors courses and continued to receive high grades. Though she described much of her coursework as meaningless and irrelevant, Connie confessed to her joy in outguessing her instructors at exam time. She viewed her college experiences as her way of playing "The Big Game."

Connie had no counseling experiences prior to her visit to the counseling center. When she had felt troubled and upset in the past, she had talked about her problems with Father Anthony. Connie said that she came to the center because she had "lost touch with herself" and felt constantly depressed. For the past four days she had left her room at night and wandered around the streets and sidewalks of the university until dawn. She often rested and sought refuge in the darkened balcony of the Catholic church. Connie reported that when she got back to her room, she couldn't remember where she had been or what she had done.

INITIAL COUNSELING INTERVIEW

During the first therapy session Connie displayed a large amount of confused thinking and behavior. Her poor physical condition underscored her inability to focus her thoughts on any topic of importance to her. She began by saying that she had been receiving "bad vibrations" from her roommates and that her family had recently been "out of sight." Immediately following the information, Connie gave an intellectualized discourse on the topic of the nonworth of higher education. She concluded her discussion with the comment, "But nothing has answers anyway," and her nervous, high-pitched giggling. Then she lapsed into silence and gazed down at the floor.

After a few moments of this, Connie abruptly indicated her concern that her therapist might think that she didn't have any serious problems after all, and throw her out. She said:

Like, I'm hurting inside my head, you know. It's like I'm listening to self-destruct messages. Really weird stuff . . . and it's got me spooked. I'm a loner—always have been, you know. It's

69

*the natural scene for me. Normally I don't give a damn who likes
me and who doesn't. They can buzz off. But lately nobody
seems tuned in on my wavelength or anything. They're tuning
me out. I don't even like myself. Sounds crazy, right? Wow! All
those bad vibes.*

The therapist had purposefully been quiet while trying to understand and interpret Connie's behavior. He responded, "Connie, you can
come here as long as you feel there is a need. *You* decide, or we can
mutually decide, when you have come long enough." This particular
response had an important impact on Connie. The therapist later
learned that his invitation for continued therapy and the emphasis on
her involvement in the therapeutic process, tentatively caused Connie
to trust him. Much later Connie told him that if he had tried to "moral-
ize her" in the first session, she would have left his office and never
come back.

The first therapy session ended when Connie agreed to a verbal
contract with her therapist to come back for two more hour-long sessions. He pointed out that it would take them at least that long to identify the source of her problems. Connie answered by jumping up from
her chair and quickly walking to the door. She opened the door and
turned back to the therapist, saying:

*Yeah, I'll come back. Maybe I need a shrink. Maybe you can
help me get my head straight. Sort things out. See you first thing
in the morning, if I'm not crashing. . . .*

When Connie came into his office the next morning, it was obvious
that she was physically and emotionally upset. Her bleary red eyes and
tear-streaked face told her story; she had wandered aimlessly all night in
the rain. She wore the same clothes and her hair was matted. She had
lost her shoes somewhere in the night. After entering the office, Connie
paced slowly around the room. The therapist took his chair and quietly
watched her. After several minutes he began, "Want to talk?" She answered:

*Like, you can't understand me at all! You can't get into it
with me because you're too damn straight. You sit in here and
pretend you're different. Like you've got a handle on how to live
or something. But you don't really care. You've never been high
or turned on by anything. It's like talking to a statue about how*

70

flowers smell. It's like you can live and die and not live at all,
you know. Take me. I'm not living at all. I'm nowhere, man,
nowhere. . . .

Connie's eyes and facial expression reflected the tone of defeat in her
voice. After she finished talking she sat quietly in the chair, emotionally
exhausted. Her therapist recognized that her thoughts were confused.
She was displaying resentment toward him as a member of the estab-
lishment and frustration over her need to seek his professional help. He
also recognized that Connie had an approach-avoidance conflict about
her need for therapy to regain emotional stability. Her internal struggle
seemed to center on not being able to understand her own self-defeating behavior. He decided to share his feelings about Connie's ambivalent
behavior toward his offer of help:

> *I'm feeling frustrated, Connie. Yesterday you walked in here*
> *and told me that you were feeling bad vibes and thinking about*
> *death all the time. . . . You said you wanted my help. But today*
> *you seem to be pushing against the idea that you need help,*
> *especially from me.*
>
> *I get the feeling that you really haven't begun to level with*
> *me . . . or yourself. You've told me about how bad your parents*
> *and sister are, but you haven't talked about how bad you feel.*
> *That's important to me. We really aren't working toward any-*
> *thing yet. My hunch is that you're afraid to open up . . . to tell*
> *me how you really feel . . . inside. That's how I feel. How do you*
> *feel, Connie?*

Connie answered, "I feel spaced out and numb. . . . Spooked about
seeing a shrink. . . . Like I'm really crashing bad this time." Then she
closed her eyes, mumbled a few more words, and dropped into fitful
sleep.

Her therapist understood the desperate need for sleep. He decided
to call the Psychiatric Intern at the student infirmary to see if he could
have Connie admitted to the ward for a physical examination and psychological observation. He was fortunate; an appointment was con-
firmed for that afternoon. After a few minutes he woke Connie and
explained what he had done. He pointed out to her that it was very
important for both of them to know if she was physically ill or not. She
seemed to accept what he said and agreed to keep the appointment at

71

the infirmary. Connie left his office with a promise to come back in a few days. He didn't see her again for three weeks.

Analysis of the information offered by Connie during her first two therapy sessions indicated that she was experiencing serious emotional and psychological conflict. Three significant problem areas were: (1) lack of purpose in her life, (2) feelings of parental rejection, and (3) ineffective personal relationships. It seemed apparent that her problems of alienation in these areas were closely related and often mutually reinforced her high anxiety level. Connie was unable to cope effectively with her complex problems and was making use of maladaptive behavior.

COUNSELING METHODOLOGY

Existential counseling theory is often difficult to comprehend because it has evolved from diverse origins. Theologically oriented scholars such as Kierkegaard and Tillich, philosophical writers like Heidegger and Sartre, and psychological advocates like May and Frankl have all added substantially to the formulation of existential thought. Beck (1963) has indicated that counseling theorists have found value in their adaptation of an existential view of life to the counseling process. Existential counseling is essentially viewed as a process of making the client free. May (1961) described personal freedom as essentially an "inner thing"—something which exists in the living person aside from any of the outward choice of alternatives that many of us think of as constituting freedom:

> No matter how great the forces victimizing the human being, man has the capacity to know that he is being victimized, and thus to influence in some way how he will relate to his fate. There is never lost that kernel of the power to take some stand, to make some decision, no matter how minute.

In describing the existential approach to psychotherapy, May (1961) wrote:

> It is not a system of therapy, but an attitude toward therapy, not a set of new techniques but a concern with the understanding of the structure of the human being and his experience that must underlie all techniques.

72

A primary concern of the existential therapist is the expression of his client's efforts to find meaning in his life. Frankl (1955) identified the source of mental disturbance as an individual's inability to find meaning in his life rather than traumatic life experiences that shape the personality. He developed the concept of "existential neurosis" to explain how man becomes alienated and isolated in a rapidly changing world. The existential approach to psychology works against fractionating the elements of man's behavior in an attempt to understand and predict. Instead, a holistic approach is used to grasp the total reality and essence of the individual client. Each expression of the client is viewed as part of his whole being and as a developmental stage in the lifelong process of becoming.

Existential psychologists assume that the most fundamental characteristic of man is his existence, his individual understanding of the external world around him. His feelings, desires, guilt, and anxiety are caught up in his world of personal meaning. Each time he experiences an event, he places his interpretation of that event somewhere in his system of meaning. The meaning in a man's private world determines his behavior. Existential logic suggests that if the therapist could know the world in which his client lives, he would know him.

Another basic concept of existential psychology is the idea that each individual has unlimited potential for growth. The human being is not viewed as a static entity; he is seen as being in a constant state of evolution, transition, and becoming. His psychological development is closely linked to his ability to successfully integrate subsequent experiences from the external world. Existential psychologists share the conviction that man actualizes himself, or fulfills his inner potentials, by participation in dialogue with other men. Some qualities of being human can be developed only in relation to another person. To understand himself, man needs to be understood; by being understood, man learns to understand. The therapist's purpose is to facilitate the client's process of becoming by allowing him to gain knowledge of himself in therapeutic encounter.

A third distinctive characteristic of existential therapy is the central issue of death. Being implies the fact of nonbeing, and the meaning of existence involves the fact of nonexistence. Because man knows that at some future time he will not be, existentialists assume that the threat of nonbeing is the source of normal anxiety, since it is present in all individuals. This form of existential anxiety strikes at the center of the individual's self-concept because it represents dissolution of the self.

The ultimate goal of existential therapy is for the patient to experience his existence as real. His movement toward understanding his personal freedom is the core of the therapeutic process. The therapy leads him to become aware of his existence fully, including becoming aware of his unique potential abilities and limitations. The therapist enables the individual to see and to recognize what he has always had— choice and freedom. Binswanger (1956) clarified the goals of therapy when he wrote:

> *Therapy proceeds not merely by showing the patient where, when, and to what extent he has failed to realize the fullness of his humanity, but tries to make him experience this as radically as possible. . . .*

Because primary importance is placed upon gaining entry into the individual's life space, existential psychologists have relegated methods and techniques of therapy to a position of secondary importance. There seems to be no established methodological approach to accomplish existential psychotherapy and counseling; techniques vary according to the personality of the therapist. What remains the same is the understanding that the basic task is to enter the client's world and participate with him in its realities. The personal existence of the therapist is a major tool in helping the client. Emphasis is placed on the importance of the *self* of the therapist rather than his techniques. His ability to be human and genuine enables the client to become aware of similar qualities in himself. Through this process the client will realize his ability for self-growth.

The basic approach to creating an existential relationship is to encourage the client to focus his thoughts on immediate feelings of self-awareness. In this manner the therapist allows his client freedom to choose the subject matter of therapy. The spontaneity and lack of structure in the therapy situation make it possible for the client to reveal his mode of being-in-the-world. The anxiety that caused the client to bury his awareness of parts of his own existence finds expression in an atmosphere of acceptance and consideration.

As the client begins to talk about his feelings and his understanding of his existence, the therapist is careful to listen for nonverbal messages his client might be sending.

Van Dusen (1971) described the importance of nonverbal messages:

One will not grasp the patient solely by his words (a tendency in many overly logical therapists). Features of his world are his body sensations, his use of his musculature, his gestures, his choice and use of clothes and even the inflections of voice underlying the words. Such a small matter as where he puts his gaze is quite important. Does he communicate eye-to-eye with the therapist or is he talking to a potted plant in the corner? No part of his world is so small as to be meaningless. This approach to patients implies a much richer and more subtle understanding than the simple grabbing another by his words.

The client's meaning is expressed in his behavior as well as words; it is a fruitful area for the therapist to observe as he works to communicate with his client.

Most existential therapists are not very concerned about determining the origin of the client's difficulties. They are concerned with the client as he is now, not as he was in the past. The client is not encouraged to escape his current psychological problems by returning to the fixed history of his past, where there are no decisions to be made, and there is no necessity to shape meaning out of today's experience. The focus is on the now events, those things actually happening in therapy rather than remembered or anticipated events; past and future are important only as they are related to what is happening in the present.

Van Dusen (1971) underscored the emphasis on the here-now events in therapy:

In exploring the being-in-the-world of the other, one explores the world here, now. Only insofar as past or future are tangled in the world here-now do these become of consequence. After all, his world is here-now. It's not back in toilet training in childhood or forward in afterlife. He sits here before me and demonstrates his world. . . . There isn't the long escape into what mama, papa, or sister did. We are here. What are you doing now?

The here-now quality of the relationship determines to what degree the personal world of the client will find genuine expression. The purpose of the therapist is to provide an encounter experience for mutual benefit; he and his client become existential partners in the search for meaning. In a sense, therapist and client "live" therapy because it becomes an important segment of life for each of them.

Connie's therapist was a young man who had recently completed his doctorate in counseling psychology at a large midwestern university. He and his wife had been married five years and had a three-year-old girl. He had been employed at the counseling center for two years. By nature and cognitive choice, he was an extrovert. Though he was over thirty, Connie's counselor felt that he could genuinely communicate with young people. His attitude was straightforward, honest, and sincere, with the recognition that it was not possible to solve everyone's problems. He chose existential counseling methods because they best suited his style of life, and they gave him a chance to work with the immediate questions raised by the young people of Connie's generation.

Three weeks after Connie failed to keep her hastily arranged appointment at the infirmary, her therapist received a phone call from Father Anthony. He learned that Connie had been admitted to the infirmary after she had collapsed on the front steps of the church that morning. She had spent another night in the darkened balcony. Connie apparently had not eaten for several days and was suffering from malnutrition and physical exhaustion.

The counselor visited Connie in the infirmary and found it difficult to recognize her as the same girl he had seen before. Her skin was unusually pale and her eyes seemed to be sunken in her head. He later described her in his therapy notes as "removed and very distant, almost as if she wasn't really inside her body." Connie spoke in a very depressed, flat voice about being lonely and having taken a trip "to the dark side of her soul." Her speech was disjointed and incoherent. Much of what Connie talked about was the certainty of death and her ability to accept her own death as a natural event. She framed her problems in nihilistic terms: "There's no reason to do anything about how bad you feel, man, because nothing really matters but death, anyway . . . you know."

Connie's therapist sensed that underlying what she was saying was a desperate attempt to find someone she could communicate with about something of value to hold on to. She seemed to be searching for something logical that she could understand and believe. Because he was worried about the possibility of a psychotic break with reality, he decided to make daily visits to see Connie in the infirmary. The sessions would not be in the normal form of therapy, but would focus on helping Connie gain feelings of worth and trust in herself.

During his second visit with Connie the counselor began to recognize the restrictions for communication set by Connie. She allowed their discussion of her feelings to progress only to a certain emotional depth. When they reached a sensitive area that made her feel anxious, she stopped responding and confronted him with a blank stare. He interpreted her nonverbal message to mean, "If you make me feel uptight about what I've done, I'll just tune you out and go back into my private mental world. Nobody can give me a rough time in there." He decided to translate his covert feelings into a statement:

> *Connie . . . as we work together, I'm trying to help you search your inner world for understanding. But I'm still a person. I risk myself and let myself go with you. Most of what I say is based on my sensitivity to you and what you are feeling. I want to share my feelings and vague images of what may be happening between us. Right now, I feel like you're trying to prove that I can't help you . . . that I really don't care about you. . . . Then you would be safe in rejecting me and hiding in your head. Is that what you're feeling?*

What the therapist said had a remarkable effect on Connie. Though she said very little during the rest of the session, she seemed more receptive to him.

At the beginning of the third session in the infirmary Connie was able to say:

> *Last time you were asking me about where I got my personal strength. If you meant religion, no. That's out. I really don't go that route. But I've got a little different perspective from this bed.*
>
> *Like I've been thinking about what you said. You put some pretty heavy stuff on me. . . . The part about being very manipulative and self-destructive. I guess you're right about some of it. Like my saying life isn't worth living, I make other people argue that it is. Then I destroy them with logic and examples. Show them where it's at, you know. But that's a bad trip because I'm really cutting myself down . . . a bad scene. But I still don't have it together yet. . . .*

Connie seemed to understand that she often set up situations that alienated people around her and reinforced her feelings of inadequacy.

Two days later Connie appeared in her therapist's office late in the afternoon and demanded to see him without an appointment. It became apparent to him that Connie was very agitated and upset. She paced the floor rapidly and began to sob uncontrollably. Twenty minutes passed before Connie gained enough self-control to allow her therapist to administer some relaxation techniques. After helping Connie to release some of her physical tension, he began to explore the immediate events that prompted her unscheduled visit.

Connie began by explaining that since they had talked that morning many things had begun to come together. She traced her intense feelings of being uptight to the fact that she was about to have a birthday. As far back as Connie could remember, her birthdays were very unhappy days. She said that usually her mother got drunk and accused her father of an affair with another woman. Her mother would say to Connie, depending on Connie's age, "Seventeen years ago today, I was in the hospital having you, while your father was sneaking around having an affair with another woman. When I needed your father the most, he wasn't there." Connie's father defended himself by arguing that the extramarital affair was ancient history and that he had been faithful to his wife since confessing the affair. Connie said that she spent almost every birthday night hiding under her bed crying. She retreated into a fantasy world where she saw herself far away from home where everything was clean and peaceful. She said that she usually dreamed about being on a long lonely stretch of beach somewhere with the hot sun shining directly on her.

As she continued to talk about her terrible birthdays, Connie became more and more upset. Her voice carried rising momentum as she said, "I have *never* been loved. My parents *never* cared anything about me. My birthdays have *always* been drunken horrible messes." She sat on the edge of the chair and clenched her fists. In her desperate need to strike out at something, she began to brutally pound her legs, repeating the phrases, "I have *never* been loved, *never* been wanted. . . . They have *never* loved me. . . ." After a considerable length of time Connie slumped back into the chair and cried quietly.

The counselor responded to her agony by moving close to her and placing his hand gently on her shoulder. He said:

> *I feel very close to you now Connie. We are closer than we have ever been before. . . . I want to help you. . . . Any human being at one time or another recognizes the loneliness in his life. Somehow we have to come to grips with it in our own way.*

> *If we're lucky, we might find someone we can share our innermost thoughts with . . . you know, our doubts, our fears,*

and maybe our joys. That's really special. But even the closest relationship can't eliminate the feeling of being alone in this world. Carrying our own load is tough. That's the only answer I've found.

Early the next morning Connie returned for her scheduled appointment and told her counselor that she was not going to go home for her birthday. She said that she had come to realize that she never wanted to see her family again. She had mailed a letter to her parents saying that she was not going to come home anymore. The therapist encouraged Connie to concentrate on what she was feeling when she wrote the letter. He asked her, "What was going on inside? Where were you at?" Connie began:

> *I don't know if I can get into it, you know. It was weird . . . really weird. I've been messing round inside my head so long. I don't think I felt anything. Like I'm strung out and there wasn't anything there. I mean, like where were they when I needed them? All my life I can remember them fighting and drinking. No protection from it . . . you couldn't break out.*
>
> *Hey, a flashback! I just remembered that when I was a little kid, I used to draw trees and call them lonely. Just bare trees, man. Can you see it. . . ? Far out, huh? Maybe that's why I'm blowing my mind. They never saw me as a real person. . . .*

As the counselor listened to Connie talk about how her parents had treated her, he recognized that she had never developed an emotional relationship with them that was stabilized by love. Without their love and acceptance, Connie began to deny her natural feelings of affection toward them and generalized her negative feelings toward others. Connie was like a color-blind person arguing that color vision was no asset. She had stunted her emotional development by refusing to commit herself to anyone or anything. By denying herself the experience of feeling genuine emotions, Connie could not integrate valuable experiences that would give her a sense of identity. Since her parental situation was not likely to change, the counselor decided to encourage Connie to think about exploring her future.

> *Connie, if you say you don't, uhh, you choose not to belong to your past . . . is there something you would like to create?*

You once said something about drawing or painting. Is there
something in you that you'd like to share?

Connie answered:

Well, uhh, like there are little things . . . minutes when I
enjoy myself. When my head's straight, you know. I like to
write; even did some acting in high school. I'm into art stuff.
You know, the shops around campus . . . you can see where
other people's ideas are.

But I don't know . . . you know, no big deal. I don't know if
it's a part of me. Like I never really . . . it's like it doesn't mean
that much. Nothing means anything to me really. I really don't
care about anything. All I want is to stop hurting and picking up
the bad vibes, you know. . . .

OUTCOME

Connie visited her counselor for two more counseling sessions and made
limited progress toward increased self-acceptance. One of the major
factors in her improved psychological adjustment was the emotional
relief she gained from sharing her problems with a person who was
interested in her.

The counseling sessions focused primarily on her inability to cope
with the anxiety caused by feelings of loneliness and mutual rejection
between Connie and her parents. Her therapist directed his efforts
toward helping Connie learn that loneliness is a two-faced thing; it can
be a creative part of human existence or it can be something damaging
to a human—an experience in self-rejection and misery. Connie abruptly
terminated therapy by writing her counselor a hastily scribbled note
canceling further appointments because she was leaving the university
to "break out and get her head straight."

Modern man, normal as well as neurotic, is characterized by alienation from the world he lives in. Existential therapy and counseling
move the philosophical issues of man's goals, values, and existence to
the forefront of the helping relationship. They emphasize the idea that
a person's identity or awareness of himself is a basic antecedent of his behavior. This was true for Connie. Her sense of alienation seemed to over-
power her need to develop emotional bonds with those who knew her.

FOCUS QUESTIONS

1. This case demonstrated the elusive problems of the human heart and psyche in conflict with itself. Many young people are struggling with problems of identity, alienation, and existential anxiety. How can therapists and counselors help them as they struggle for personal meaning?

2. Connie's therapist made use of existential counseling methods to supply the integrating experiences that might have given her a sense of identity and connectedness to others. What alternative counseling methods might have accomplished the same goals?

3. Existential psychologists emphasize the fact that each individual is constantly confronted by choices and decisions, with the consequent responsibility which they entail. They also place great emphasis on the here-now quality of the counseling experience. How does this differ from other counseling approaches?

4. Existential psychology places special recognition on the depth and seriousness of human life and of the place of anxiety in it. Does this make it uniquely applicable to contemporary America?

5. In this case the existential methods of the therapist and the nature of Connie's problems fortunately coincided. What if this was not the case?

6. Through counseling, Connie was offered a human relationship that carried some hope of growth and change for her. Would you consider the therapist ineffectual because of Connie's abrupt termination? What do you think the therapist felt as he read Connie's note?

7. The terms therapy and counseling were used interchangeably in this case study. Which term do you feel more appropriate? What criteria would you use to make your decision?

8. How much would the existential therapist profit from a brief period of self-reflection after each therapy session as he asked himself: What did we work on? What was I feeling? Was I uneasy, excited, or relaxed? Was anything said that threatened me? How did that session affect me? What am I feeling now?

BIBLIOGRAPHY: CONNIE

Beck, Carlton E. *Philosophical Foundations of Guidance.* Englewood Cliffs, N.J.: Prentice-Hall, 1963.

Binswanger, L. "Existential Analysis and Psychotherapy." In Fromm-Reichmann, Frieda, and Moreno, J. L., eds. *Progress in Psychotherapy.* New York: Grune and Stratton, 1956.

Frankl, V. E. *The Doctor and the Soul.* New York: Alfred A. Knopf, 1955.

_____. "On Logotherapy and Existential Analysis," *American Journal of Psychoanalysis* 18, no. 1 (1958), pp. 28–37.

May, Rollo. *Existential Psychology.* New York: Random House, 1961.

_____. "Freedom and Responsibility Re-examined." Unpublished paper given at American Personnel and Guidance Association Convention, Chicago, 1962.

Van Dusen, Wilson. "Existential Analytic Psychotherapy." In Beck, Carlton E., ed. *Philosophical Guidelines For Counseling.* Dubuque, Iowa: William C. Brown, 1971.

CRITIQUE OF THE CASE OF CONNIE

The existential counseling approach to the case of Connie seems quite relevant as a method of treating her. She obviously appeared to lack a purpose for being, and this was reflected in her basic feelings of loneliness and worthlessness. Let us, nevertheless, critique the counselor's procedures.

Based on Connie's condition during the first interview, it would seem that the counselor should have immediately scheduled a physical examination for her. Depression (possibly suicidal), delusions, withdrawal, and the indications of loss of contact with reality, as well as signs suggesting possible use of drugs, should have been enough data to take immediate steps to protect Connie's physical well-being. This, of course, was done during the second interview when her physical condition virtually demanded immediate attention. Although the case data made no reference to the probability that Connie might have been using drugs, much of her behavior suggested that she could have been, and for this reason also a physical examination seems called for following the first interview.

It is difficult to find much to criticize in the therapist's approach beyond the interventions suggested above. Obviously he was trying to be helpful. The evidence of some of the protocol reproduced and the sequence of the interviews make it appear that the therapist did quite a bit of confronting within the second interview. This was rather risky, but evidently Connie was able to accept most of it, and it gave her some understanding of her self-destructive and manipulative behavior. Nevertheless, she did break off the relationship abruptly and left the university. Perhaps the therapist was "coming on too strong" for her, and she left because the relationship became too threatening. The therapist's silence on a couple of occasions was followed by outbursts from Connie, suggesting that the therapist needed to communicate more empathy since her outbursts were attempts to let him know where she was coming from.

Discussion Questions

1. The fact that Connie's basic problem was a deep loneliness suggests that Glasser's reality therapy (in press) might have been a good alternate model to use. Simulate by role-playing the first interview with Connie using the reality therapy model.

2. The type of problem faced by Connie is ordinarily considered least amenable to behavioral modification therapy. What elements in Connie's problem would make it difficult for treatment through behavior modification?
3. Would Connie be a good prospect for group therapy? Why or why not?

Bibliography: Critique of Connie

Glasser, William. "Reality Therapy in Groups." In Gazda, George M., ed. *Basic Approaches to Group Psychotherapy and Group Counseling,* Second Edition. Springfield, Ill.: Charles C Thomas, 1974.

III

Adults

Joanne

The male adolescent voice outside the open door of her classroom
yelled, "Hey you, honkie . . . you white bitch!" Then she heard his
running footsteps and laughter as he fled down the hall. Joanne turned
from the window and watched the upturned black faces of her ninth
grade class. Their faces registered shock, followed by curiosity, and
then restrained smiles. She knew how important her next move would
be. She smiled back at her students as she said, "Wow! That could get
an X rating easily." Nervous laughter broke out in her classroom and
the tension flowed out of the students. Soon the white teacher and her
black students joined once again in the harmony they had created during the first three weeks of school. No one, especially Joanne, quite
understood what that cry heralded for her and her students.

What began as an isolated incident in October became a daily har-
rassment routine. During sixth hour the boys would gather in the hallway outside Joanne's door and taunt her with foul names. No matter
what four letter word was used, it was prefaced by "white." Most of
the time she had no chance to retaliate. She couldn't see who was yell-
ing, and when she caught someone, she didn't know his name. An emotionally charged session with the assistant principal resulted in the sus-
pension of two students. Joanne began to feel that she couldn't fight
with her unseen enemies. As the weeks progressed, Joanne found her
teaching assignment in a predominately black school to be more and
more of a struggle. The personal fear and anxiety that she sensed, but
could not acknowledge, grew each day.

Most black students will distrust a white teacher and will hesitate to
enter into the "faith" relationship that is so necessary for good classroom interaction. Small incidents in Joanne's class illustrated the prob-

lems facing her black students. Her students seemed to like and appreciate her, but she knew they had been taught by life experiences in the ghetto to suspect everybody and to present a tough and detached appearance to the world. Torn between what they sensed and what they thought was expected from them, her students became confused. Their mixed feelings gave rise to cutting remarks about "whitey." When Joanne heard them, her self-doubts and frustration began to pile up. The more she rationalized her fears intellectually, the greater her tension grew.

A Friday morning pep assembly turned into the usual note passing and punch throwing session. Three black girls two rows down from Joanne were really getting out of hand. They were loud and defiantly throwing books as they cursed each other. Joanne felt the warm flush of color come to her neck and cheeks as she thought:

> *Why doesn't somebody do something to stop it? They are just acting like it isn't really happening. I hate to correct kids I don't know or can't appeal to. . . .*

She stood up and asked the girls to take their seats and to quiet down. The largest girl angrily said, "What you going to do if we don't, you white bitch? Huh?" Rebuffed, and knowing that she couldn't physically handle the girls, Joanne quickly tried to think of an alternative. Fortunately, the black male science teacher rescued her by coming over to discipline the girls. He sensed her precarious situation and thoughtfully sat with her for the remainder of the assembly.

After the final round of applause for the pep assembly, the students moved en masse toward the exits. Joanne walked slowly, listening to their jokes and laughter. She was thinking to herself, "I wonder how many are going to try to get through that door at once. . . ?" Suddenly she felt a sharp, breath-shattering blow to the middle of her back. She fell forward into a row of empty seats and struggled to keep from falling to the floor. She turned to face her attacker but could only see hundreds of young blacks trying to get through the exit door. She knew instinctively to go directly to the teacher's lounge. She told herself, "Walk slowly. Don't panic. Just get to the lounge." No other thoughts broke through her shock and fear.

As Joanne entered the teacher's lounge she saw her friend Susan. Susan asked, "What's wrong?" Joanne answered:

A kid hit me! Actually hit me! Nobody has ever touched me in the ten years I've been teaching . . . and now I get hit in the back by somebody I can't even see. I can't believe it. . . .

Joanne lowered her head and began to cry. Through her tears, she told Susan, "I know their life is so unfair . . . but I can't help that. I tried, but I can't take it anymore. I'm quitting." Joanne Callum, ninth grade English teacher, resigned her position that afternoon. She returned on Saturday morning to pack her personal classroom belongings and left behind ten years of excellent teaching service.

BACKGROUND

Joanne has lived in the same large city and the same lower-middle-class district all her life. With her older brother, she grew up in a home punctuated by the emotional ups and downs of her parents. Her father was a football coach and social science teacher at a large high school. When his football teams were winning, things seemed to go well at home. If his teams did poorly and his job became threatened, emotional outbursts toward his wife and children were frequent. Joanne's mother was a small, frail woman who seldom spoke out against her husband. She supplemented the family income by doing part-time recordkeeping for a cleaning service.

Joanne describes her brother Paul as "my best friend and the only real person I know. When I need him, he's there." Paul is six years older than Joanne and was a mediocre student in school. As a high school senior, he displayed great athletic ability and was selected as an all-state halfback on his father's football team. He was always well accepted by his peers and possessed a natural ability to work with others. Shortly after graduation, Paul chose to marry his girlfriend and to decline the many college athletic scholarships offered to him. A permanent family rift resulted between Paul and his father, who had previously doted on his physically gifted son. His father put it bluntly:

Such a waste. . . . He has more athletic ability in his little finger than most players. Natural God-given talent. And what does he do? He turns his back on it to get married when he's nineteen years old. . . . How can he do it? We did everything for him and he turns his back on it.

Despite his father's dire predictions of a poor marriage, Paul and his wife are still happily married twenty years later. He is currently employed as a social worker, and he and his wife have two daughters and a son.

As a child, Joanne always seemed to be socially awkward and ill-at-ease. She remembered that she never enjoyed playing with children her age; she preferred the company of older children and the women who came to visit her mother. She was an unattractive child who seemed to find her niche in life by excelling in academics. She maintained an A average in grade school and missed only one day of school in six years.

Joanne continued to be an excellent student in high school. She developed a quick wit and her intellectual ability helped her to gain membership in the National Honor Society. Though she dated infrequently, Joanne was usually accepted by her classmates in her self-chosen role as a witty but "different" student. Joanne explained that her answer to the emotional problems caused by her father was to "outthink him" and find some intellectualized escape.

Joanne's parents strongly influenced her decision to become a teacher. They repeatedly pointed out the advantages of job security and good working conditions afforded to a woman in the teaching field. They emphasized the idea that young women should go to college to be trained as teachers or to find a suitable husband, whichever happened first. Joanne chose to become an English teacher because her teachers told her that she had creative writing ability and she enjoyed the stimulation she received from reading prose and poetry.

The first year of college was a frightening time for Joanne. Freshmen were required to live in residence halls, and it was the first time she had lived apart from her parents. Joanne encountered girls with moral and social codes quite different from her own. She made few friends and had no dates. Joanne began to feel lonely and isolated from the girls she lived with, but she clung to the role of intellectual loner. She recalled:

I remember feeling like I was much older than they were. They were always playing so many silly games with each other. At times I felt like something had set me apart. . . . You know, like the planets. Apart from everybody else . . . by myself.

Joanne responded to her internal doubts by working twice as hard as other students to be sure that she got one of the highest grades in the class. She remembered that she often celebrated her academic victories alone in the college union because she had no one to share them with. For the remaining three years of college, Joanne lived with her parents and commuted to college. She continued to excel in her subjects and graduated with high honors. She described her student teaching experience as:

> *Something I had looked forward to for a long time. I wasn't disappointed, but a little surprised. The kids checked you out right away. It wasn't all subject matter and grades. I saw that I could get along well with kids and discipline was no problem. The lesson plans were easy for me and I got an A.*

For the next eight years Joanne taught ninth grade English at the large, predominately white high school where her father had coached. She learned how to develop a personal rapport with many of her students and felt secure in her classroom. She was respected by faculty members and her principal. Among her small circle of teaching friends, Joanne would have been described as "living to teach, especially those kids slow to understand or appreciate their own potential. It's her whole life."

Joanne reported that the only significant thing that she could remember occurring during those years were some "really bad" dreams. Her frightening dreams usually focused on a situation in which she "let somebody down terribly" by not doing something she should have. In these dreams she always felt insecure and would awaken in misery. She would always go into school early the next day. She explained that she just knew she would feel better if she went into school early the next morning. Joanne had become the kind of person who felt compelled to do nice things for others. If she paid a visit to a friend, she always took along some expensive liquor or a pleasant personal gift. Because she worried about how people would accept her, she always made it a package deal—Joanne and a nice gift. She usually got invited back.

Two years ago Joanne's parents were both killed in a tragic automobile accident. Joanne was sitting in the back seat of the car; her father was driving when he failed to make a rain-slickened curve on a dark night. The car crashed through the guardrail, slid down into a steep ditch, and overturned three times. The demolished car came to rest upside down against two small oak trees. In a sense, Joanne never knew what happened. In another sense, she knew everything that mattered in a vivid fraction of a second. Her father had lost control of the car and with the screeching fury of the tires, they were airborne. Then it seemed like a big explosion. She felt a flush of heat on her forehead and could hear excited shouts in the distance. When she heard the wailing cry of a police siren, she blacked out.

Joanne received a severe scalp laceration and suffered a mild concussion in the accident. Her medical tests for serious physical damage to the brain were negative. However, the examining physician pointed to the danger of undetected cerebral bleeding and ordered a week of enforced bed rest. Suddenly Joanne found herself confined to a hospital room, with the knowledge that her parents were both dead. She was not allowed to leave her bed to attend their funeral.

Those who have survived a serious accident will understand the notion that the events of the accident do not stamp themselves in memory in a sequential order. Somehow they seem to flood the mind with the fury and random impact of a tornado. Recovering from the shock of exposing your defenseless human flesh to the impact of four tons of pulverizing steel and broken glass is a gradual process. Joanne needed the healing effects of time before she gathered the strength to re-examine her memory of the accident. She began to recall the details of the accident as she might remember the parts of a long-forgotten nightmare. She was bewildered by insurance investigators who asked her to describe the accident in an orderly sequence of cause and effect, beginning to end. She still can't describe the accident accurately.

After a brief period of convalescence at her brother's home, Joanne began living alone in the house her parents had willed to her. She returned to her classroom duties and found comfort in knowing that many of her students had missed her. Soon she found herself working hard and long on the never-ending tasks associated with teaching school. The remainder of Joanne's ninth year of teaching was uneventful, except that she began to experience severe recurring headaches.

Joanne began to prepare for her next year's teaching assignment during her summer vacation period. This time she knew it would be different. New state and local plans for accelerated integration and the crosstown busing of black students in the fall would change the status of her school from predominantly white to that of predominantly black. Joanne was worried about how well she could work with black students, but chose to remain in the classroom she had come to know so well. She explained:

> *I was extremely security oriented. I think I stayed because I knew exactly what was expected of me. Starting a new job and meeting new people—that wasn't for me. I didn't want to give up the ship and transfer out to the suburbs like several of my friends did. I had the idea that fate was controlling my life, and I went along with it.*

During the past twenty years, the city where Joanne lived had received many black people from southern farms and rural towns. As the impoverished blacks moved in, the affluent whites moved out. For the first time in its history, the city lost population in 1960, and then again in 1970. Industry moved to the north and west. Department stores, services, and entertainment facilities had deserted the city and moved to the new shopping centers in the suburbs. The class structure shifted, and the taxes climbed while the tax base shrank.

The house Joanne lives in is only a block from an expressway that carries cars from one suburban outpost to another. On her block, only a few of the brick row houses evidence the owners' intentions of permanency by the investment of new paint and careful upkeep. Joanne continues to live in her house because she feels that she has no place else to go.

INITIAL COUNSELING INTERVIEW

Three months after Joanne resigned her teaching position, she had become a recluse. She seldom ventured out of her house unless it was a necessary trip to buy groceries or to visit her doctor. She often kept the draperies drawn in her living room so that, when the doorbell rang, she could peek out to see who was intruding. For Joanne, answering the door depended on whether she was psychologically ready to visit with people—most often she was not. She seldom talked with her teaching friends and often developed a headache if they dropped by to see her. Joanne had also begun the annoying habit of calling Paul or his wife twice a day to talk about her imaginary illnesses or the "heavy responsibility of keeping up the house like mom and dad would have wanted."

Paul contacted the family physician, Dr. Whitaker, and learned that a month earlier he had conducted extensive physical examinations to find a cause for the low back pain and severe headaches that Joanne reported. The tests had been negative. Dr. Whitaker mentioned to Paul that he had suggested to Joanne that her problems might be psychosomatic in origin and that perhaps she should seek psychiatric help. Dr. Whitaker had prescribed antidepressant drugs for Joanne to help her combat her occasional depression and to ward off headaches which could be caused by nervous tension. Paul visited Joanne and encouraged her to seek professional help to work on some of her problems. He recommended a psychologist in private practice that he knew to be competent and successful. Joanne agreed to go.

Joanne entered the psychologist's plushly carpeted office and sat down in the comfortable chair he offered to her. As he reviewed the form she had filled out in the waiting room, she cautiously looked at the modernistic paintings on his wall. He began the session by asking her to tell him why she was there. Joanne answered:

> *Well, I'm not sure. Dr. Whitaker said I should come. But maybe I don't really belong here. He said I should talk to you about my problems . . . , but they don't seem very important now. You see, I uhh . . . , well, I resigned my teaching position— three months and a week ago—and I haven't been feeling well. I seem to be tired all the time and I have these terrific headaches. . . . That's it. That's what my problem is.*
>
> *Look . . . I've never done this before and, as you can see, it upsets me. I don't know what is supposed to happen next. I've never been very good at talking about my feelings to anybody . . . I probably won't be very good at it. For all I know, you might have a couch hidden somewhere.*

Her therapist responded by explaining:

> *No, there's no couch or any special bag of tricks. What happens next is that I try to get you to talk about your feelings and what you think prompts them. I'll try to get you to loosen up so I can hear you talk about what is bothering you. Then maybe we can talk a little bit about what you can expect from me and from therapy.*
>
> *That's what I like to do during the first session. Sort of get to know you and understand how you look at things. Why don't*

*you just relax a little more and talk about something that is very
important to you. I'll just listen to you. . . .*

Joanne followed his instructions and tentatively began to describe
some of her feelings. She said:

> *The main thing, right now. . . . What has been on my mind
> lately, is that my body is. . . . Uhh, well it seems to be falling
> apart on me. Now before you get that "crazy for sure" look in
> your eye, let me explain something. Two years ago I was in a bad
> accident. My mother and father were killed. I got a scalp lacera-
> tion and a bad concussion. And, umm . . . well, it seems like I've
> been having problems ever since.*
>
> *Since the accident, everything seems to be changing so fast.
> It's like everything in my life is out of focus. I'm not sure where
> to begin. . . . I've been having lower back pain and cramps for
> some time now, along with these unbelievable headaches. Then
> this year I quit my teaching job because I couldn't stand the
> tension with black students anymore. . . . I went to see Doctor
> Whitaker, but he can't find anything physically wrong with me. I
> just feel so tired and rundown all the time. Anyway, he seems to
> think that I need psychiatric help—your help—to get rid of my
> headaches. My brother Paul thinks I need help, too. That's why
> I'm here. . . .*

For the next twenty or thirty minutes, Joanne continued to talk
about her physical complaints, her lack of energy, stomach upsets, and
headaches. She said that she had not actively sought another teaching
position or any other kind of work because of her "nerves." As Joanne
talked about some of her problems, her therapist became aware that her
physical fatigue had its psychological counterpart in feelings of inadequacy, low tolerance for stress, and a high level of anxiety. He made a
mental note of the fact that her face had the most expression when she
was talking about negative past experiences. Joanne didn't touch on her
present or future opportunities. It was as if, in Joanne's mind, her life
had entered a stage of suspended animation when she stopped teaching.

Joanne's therapist led toward the end of the first session by asking
her to talk about what she expected from therapy. She said that the
most rewarding thing would be to understand why she felt tired all the
time and to get rid of her headaches. He told her that unless there was a

physiological cause for her illnesses, he felt confident that they could work together to eliminate them. He closed the first session by asking Joanne for a verbal commitment to participate in at least five therapy sessions in order to give him a chance to help her. Joanne agreed.

Immediately after the first therapy session, Joanne's therapist recorded the following impressions in his notebook:

Chief Complaint: "Body falling apart," severe headaches, low back pain; referred by Dr. Whitaker who reports negative results from physical exam

Historical Development: Strong parental influence; auto accident two years ago—parents killed, concussion (trauma?) seems to have penetrated her psychological defenses; quit teaching 3 months ago; teaching and working with students very important

Diagnostic Impression: Possible anxiety neurosis, developed as reaction to sudden death of parents; new teaching situation with black students, self-doubts; intelligent but self-deceiving, seems to lack emotional warmth and depth, plays "head games", hypochondriasis (?), enjoys poor health—headaches as adaptive mechanism

COUNSELING METHODOLOGY

One of the most distinctive aspects of being human is the potential for establishing a relationship with another person. It can be a tremendously creative experience in sharing excitement, joy, and a sense of caring. When these feelings are communicated well, we fulfill ourselves by clarifying our own identity. To the extent that our relationships reflect friendship, love, and concern for others, we are becoming more human.

Along with their continued interest in the material things of "the good life," many people are now reaching out to learn more about expressing their human potential. Employers are studying how to work with their subordinates, husbands and wives are learning to "fight fair," and parents are going back to school to learn better ways to raise their children. Many people are eager to learn more about the why and how of their communication processes.

A new approach to understanding people and their behavioral expression is called Transactional Analysis. Transactional Analysis (TA) is a counseling theory first described by Dr. Eric Berne in his book, *Games People Play* (1964), and promoted by Thomas Harris' popular work, *I'm OK—You're OK* (1969). Dr. Berne has indicated that his theory developed as he watched behavioral changes which took place in a patient when a new stimulus such as a word, gesture, or sound was introduced. These changes included different facial expressions, body movements, and physical gestures. It was as though the individual had several different people inside; at any given time, one or the other of the "people" inside dominated the individual's thoughts and behavior.

Dr. Berne also observed that the different "selves" of an individual transacted with other people in different ways and that these personal transactions could be objectively studied. We saw that some of the behavioral transactions had ulterior motives; the individual used them as a means of manipulating others into psychological games. Dr. Berne reported that some of his clients seemed to perform their eccentric behavior in stylized ways, as if they were acting on a stage and following a theatrical script. These insights helped Berne to develop the basic concepts of TA theory: Parent, Adult, and Child, transaction, stroke, basic life position, and script.

One of the first important things that one notices as he learns about TA is its unique vocabulary. TA theorists have tried to move away from unclear words and psychological jargon that might confuse and alienate their clients. Vague words and concepts like ego strength, self-actualization, and interpersonal effectiveness have been replaced by words that are simple and direct. For example, the major parts of an individual's personality are called Parent, Adult, and Child.

Harris (1967) claims that TA gives a troubled person a rational method for analyzing his own behavior; it helps him operationalize information that was only dealt with before on a cognitive level. Harris points out that the contemporary language of TA makes it easier for the client and therapist to talk about the feelings behind personal behavior and to understand each other clearly.

TA theory begins with the assumption that everyone has three parts, or persons, within himself—a Parent, an Adult, and a Child. These parts are technically called ego states. Berne (1964) defined an ego state as "a consistent pattern of feeling and experience related to a corresponding consistent pattern of behavior." Berne partially based his definition on the work of Dr. Penfield (1952), a neurosurgeon who demonstrated that an electronic probe applied to different parts of the brain would evoke memories and feelings long forgotten by the individual. Berne wrote:

> *In this respect the brain functions like a tape recorder to preserve complete experiences in serial sequence, in a form recognizable as "ego states"—indicating that ego states comprise the natural way of experiencing and recording experiences in their totality.*

Berne concluded that everything that happens to a person is somehow recorded and stored in his brain. This would include all childhood experiences, information and feelings from parents, and individual perceptions of the surrounding world. Also included would be the feelings that were associated with the original events and the distortions that a person attached to his memories. These "memory tapes" could be recalled or replayed by the individual when he found himself in a situation similar to his previous experience.

James and Jongeward (1971) have offered a working definition of the three ego states relevant to TA:

Parent Ego State: Contains the attitudes and behavior incorporated from external sources, primarily parents. Outwardly, it often is expressed toward others in prejudicial, critical, and nurturing behavior. Inwardly, it is experienced as old parental messages which continue to influence the inner child.

Adult Ego State: Is not related to a person's age. It is oriented to current reality and the objective gathering of information. It is organized, adaptable, intelligent, and functions by testing reality, estimating probabilities, and computing dispassionately.

Child Ego State: Contains all the impulses that come naturally to an infant. It also contains the recordings of his early experiences, how he responded to them, and the "positions" he took about himself and others. It is expressed as "old" (archaic) behavior from childhood.

They go on to point out that when you are acting, thinking, or feeling as you observed your parents to be doing, you are in your Parent Ego State. When you are dealing with current reality, gathering facts, and computing objectively, you are in your Adult Ego State.

When you are feeling and acting as you did when you were a child, you are in your Child Ego State.

The three ego states can also be described as three different voices inside the individual. The Parent would be represented by a directive voice that says, "Don't," "Never," "Always," and "You should." The adult voice would require that the individual operate only on facts, not feelings. An Adult voice would say, "I want to go to the show and out for dinner, but I can't afford to do both." The Child voice would offer spontaneous comments like, "She stinks," or "I hate homework." These voices interact frequently in interpersonal situations.

The special TA word used to describe how people talk and interact with each other is *transaction*. A transaction is an exchange between two people. It can be an exchange of friendly words or angry shouts. When one person sends a message to another, he expects a response. If you say "Hello" to someone, and he replies "Good morning," you have completed a transaction. In a sense, the Parent, Adult, or Child in the other person was responding to your Parent, Adult, or Child, depending on how you said "Hello." Diagram 1 shows examples of simple, parallel transactions. The lines with arrows indicate the direction of communication; they are called parallel transactions because the lines of communication do not cross.

A second kind of transaction is illustrated in Diagram 2. Here the lines of communication have become crossed, resulting in a breakdown of open communication.

Another key TA concept is the *stroke*. A stroke can be positive (a pleasant compliment from a friend) and helps you feel that you are OK, or negative (a critical memo from your boss) and tells you that you are not OK. Everyone needs some kind of stroking, pleasant or unpleasant. As an individual grows up, he may be willing to substitute word stroking ("you're a good boy") for the physical stroking of childhood. Both physical and verbal stroking remain important for the individual throughout life.

According to TA theory, the way the Child of the individual feels about himself and other people is called a *basic life position.* McCormick and Campos (1969) have identified the four basic life positions:

1. *I'm OK—You're OK.* This is the only healthy position.
2. *I'm OK—You're not OK.* This is a distrustful position. It is a position taken by a Child who is suspicious of people.

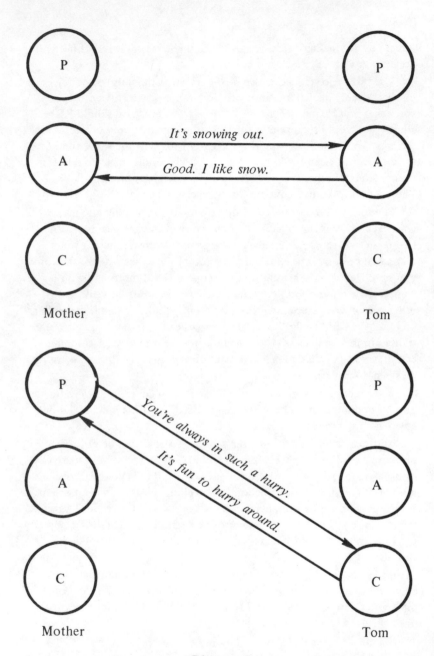

Diagram 1

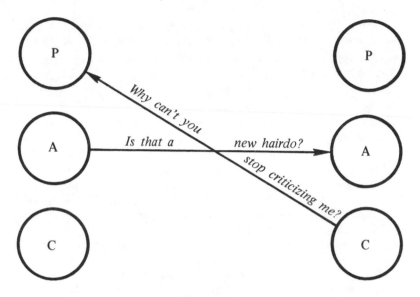

Diagram 2

3. *I'm not OK—You're OK.* This is the position of the Child who usually feels low or depressed.
4. *I'm not OK—You're not OK.* This is the position of a Child who feels that life just isn't any good, and he may even go crazy to escape it.

As the individual adopts one of the four basic life positions described above, he begins to create his *script,* the design the individual places on situations that occur in his life. A script can be defined briefly as the life plan. It is similar to a dramatic stage script in that the individual feels compelled to play it out during his transactions with others. The person's script reflects early feelings that he experienced as a child and recorded in his Child Ego State. For example, you as a Child may have decided that it wasn't quite OK to achieve more than your siblings because your parents told you a brother or sister always seemed to accomplish more than you did. In order to understand the script you use to respond to life situations, TA theory offers the process of *script analysis.* Studying your script is the process of learning about the basic life position you have assumed in your relationships with others. In fulfilling the script, you develop psychological games to support the self-image you want to project to others.

Berne (1967) defined a psychological game as "a recurring set of transactions, often repetitive, superficially rational, with a concealed motivation; or, more colloquially, as a series of transactions with a gimmick." A game is something like a "put-on" in that the message to the other person has a secret or hidden purpose. Psychological games are played to win, but a person who plays games as a way of life is usually not a winner. Here is an example of a popular game called "Now I've Got You."

> *It is Saturday afternoon, and you have invited some friends over to watch an important local college football game. You notice that Susan is not enjoying the game. (You never did like her very much.) When the game is over, and everyone else is talking about it, you might say to Susan, "Did you like the game?" (You already know she doesn't understand football and wasn't watching it.) Susan answers, "No. And I don't understand why you men go for all that violence." This gives you a chance to complete your game and get a psychological payoff by saying, "You know, Susan, you're the only wife who didn't like it. What's wrong with you anyway?"*

James and Jongeward (1971) have identified three important elements that should be present to characterize transactions as games rather than normal relationships:

1. An ongoing series of complementary transactions which are plausible on the social level
2. An ulterior (hidden) transaction which is the underlying message of the game
3. A predictable payoff which concludes the game and is the real purpose for playing

The games people play prevent honest, open, and worthwhile relationships between the players. People play them because they provoke attention, reinforce early opinions about others, and reinforce their thoughts about their own basic life position. The kinds of games people choose to play and the frequency with which they play them reflect the basic life positions they have adopted.

In summary then, TA is a tool that the individual can use to know himself, understand how he relates to others, and explore his potential for self-growth. As the individual creates an awareness of his three ego states, he becomes more able to distinguish the sources of his thoughts, feelings, and behavior patterns. He can see more clearly where there is friction and harmony within his own personality.

As the individual analyzes his transactions, he can gain a more conscious control of how he affects others and how they seek to change him. He can determine when his transactions are complementary, crossed, or ulterior and discover what kinds of games he is likely to play with others.

The goal of TA therapy is to teach the client to cognitively and emotionally recognize his ego states of Parent, Adult, and Child and to help him learn about the basic life position he has assumed in his relationships with other people. It is the client's responsibility to decide whether or not he wants to change his basic life position.

Joanne's therapist is a middle-aged man who completed his doctorate in clinical psychology at a large southern university. He has taught as a college professor in the psychology department at a university for fifteen years. Currently he is a state-licensed psychologist and has been in private practice in the city for six years. He and his wife have been married twenty-six years and have raised two sons and a daughter.

Joanne's counselor is a mature, warm, and sincere person with the awareness that he cannot solve everyone's problems. His approach to therapy is straightforward and direct. During his years of private practice he has continued to look for effective and practical counseling methods. Three years ago he became familiar with TA methodology at a workshop conducted in California. He adapted TA techniques to his personal approach to therapy because he found them to be useful in explaining the mechanics of therapy to those with little knowledge of what to expect. When asked to describe this personal approach to therapy, he answered:

> I start out with the assumption that each one of us is neurotic in one sense or another. You and me . . . we all try to carry through life a set of unsolved problems, prejudices, and biased responses to the world around us. The way we try to solve our personal problems is just that—personal. So none of us are really "normal."
>
> The second point that I try to make is that I don't conduct therapy to make people feel secure. . . . I work to help them understand that they must learn to cope with anxiety and somehow to deal with it effectively. We know that all people are

insecure, some just handle it better than others. I can't promise them a feeling of security, but I can give them a chance to understand their feelings of insecurity.

Joanne's therapist described his counseling method as a combination of Transactional Analysis, humanistic psychology, and "anything else I can find to help my clients." His eclectic approach to working with people evolved from years of therapeutic interaction and his knowledge of recent developments in mental health. He explained:

> *I've tried to work out a healthy integration of the two techniques. The TA vocabulary helps me to "hook" most of my clients into working on their problems. They can understand it quickly and put it to use in their daily lives as well as in my office. I like that. It gives them a feel for what therapy is all about. Once we can both understand the therapy "game," we can move on to focus on things like self-awareness and changing their behavior.*

He said that he found TA techniques useful because they develop the client's awareness of emotional ego states and couple that awareness with a sense of self-responsibility.

The second therapy session for Joanne began when her therapist asked her, "How have you been feeling since we got together two days ago?" She answered, "Not very well at all. Nothing's changed, and I've got a splitting headache." Her body language and facial gestures underscored her complaint of physical discomfort. Her therapist asked her to begin by describing in detail some of the feelings she had experienced that morning. Joanne responded:

> *Well, I woke up and had this headachey feeling again. I felt "blah." I knew I was going to feel bad all day . . . like something was missing again. It was hot and sticky in bed and I only got a little sleep. I thought to myself, "No rest for the wicked." Then I turned over and went back to sleep. I didn't wake up until my phone started ringing at 11:30. I didn't answer it because I didn't feel like talking to anybody. I just hid my head in my pillow and waited until it stopped ringing. . . . I felt empty again. . . .*

Joanne's therapist countered:

JOANNE

> *You know, Joanne, I've been thinking about what you said
> last time . . . about your headaches and cramps . . . and I'm won-
> dering if maybe your anxiety about your health and headaches
> might be a substitute for what you really feel about yourself and
> the people around you. . . . After all, we don't usually ask some-
> one who is physically crippled or sick to compete with someone
> who is healthy and normal. . . . Maybe being sick or tired—or
> having a headache—somehow takes you out of the competition
> of life with a reasonable amount of honor. That's a strong way
> of putting it, but does some of it ring a little bit true for you?*

She answered:

> *I just don't know anymore, Doctor. . . . This may sound
> crazy, I know, but every once in a while, I can't tell whether . . .
> something is really happening to me or I'm just imagining. Some-
> times I'm afraid I'll never get hold of myself . . . like I'm slipping
> farther away into emptiness.*

Joanne's words were followed by tears.

The therapist decided to move the discussion away from Joanne's
feelings of anxiety and physical discomfort by introducing the topic of
Transactional Analysis. He began by explaining that TA was a recent
development in the mental health field. He told Joanne that he thought
it would be an effective approach for them to use to learn how to understand each other during the therapeutic hour. Joanne expressed a
willingness to try it.

For the rest of the counseling session, Joanne and her therapist
worked on helping her to understand TA vocabulary and mechanics. He
gave her a pamphlet by McCormick and Campos, *Introduce Yourself To
Transactional Analysis,* and asked her to study it before her next appointment. Joanne ended the second session by thanking him for the
pamphlet and giving him her polite practiced little smile. She let herself
out the door. He recorded in Joanne's folder: TA pamphlet; critical
shortage of warmth; parent messages: You're not OK.

Several nights later Joanne turned over in bed and put her hand to
rest on top of the wadded-up extra pillow. Suddenly she was wide
awake. Though she didn't open her eyes, she knew what was about to
happen. More than once during the two years since her parents had
died, she had experienced the same feeling of dread. Her fears filled the
darkened bedroom with images of her parents. By reaching over to turn

105

on the light, she could force them to face away from her. But somehow she also wanted her unapproving parents in the room. She knew that the visions of her parents would eventually stalk off into a ghostly silence and leave her looking at the face of the lighted clock.

Joanne thought, "Three more hours before breakfast." As she gave up trying to make out the figures on her clock, she dropped off to sleep again. She dreamed that she was walking down Wentworth Avenue in the springtime. It was early morning and she enjoyed the clear, sharp air. On the other side of the street she could see a very highbred black dog, with beautiful long hair and a disciplined step. The dog paused at each street corner in doubt, looking up at people passing by and whimpering politely to them, "Me? Me? Me?" When they did not answer, the dog went on. Joanne thought to herself, "A valuable dog like that alone on the street. It's lost. It could get hit by a car. Or someone will pick it up to steal it . . . or maybe sell it to the doctors who cut them up!"

Joanne woke up perspiring from tension and then realized that she was in her bedroom. The grey sunlight had begun to filter through the curtains. It was time to put her feet on the cold floor and begin another day. She decided to tell her dream to the therapist.

The third therapy session began with a brief rehearsal of TA language and the special meanings of certain words. Joanne was quick to grasp the language of TA and expressed a desire to talk about her recent dream.

> Well, you know there's no rest for the wicked. Last night—no, it was early this morning—I, uh, woke up and had this bad feeling. Like I was going to be sick or something. For some reason I woke up very early, but I was very tired. I didn't open my eyes, but it just seemed like my parents were in my bedroom with me. Kind of scary, you know. . . . But then I went back to sleep again and had a sad dream about this beautiful black dog. . . .

Her therapist interrupted:

> Excuse me, but I want to stop you for just a minute to check something out. When you started to tell me about your dream, what were you feeling inside? Where were you in terms of PAC?

Joanne answered:

106

I'm not sure. The first feeling I had was. . . . Words I said were about "no rest for the wicked." That seems like a Parent message. But I was feeling guilty, like a little child, about being awake so early in the morning. I didn't want to open my eyes or let my parents catch me, you know. So that seems like I was in my Child, right? I think I was feeling not OK.

Joanne went on to explain how she felt during and after her dream. Her therapist occasionally asked her what she was feeling—at that moment—and where she was in terms of PAC. He was working to develop her awareness of the emotional interaction between her three ego states. He explained that she could learn to tell which part of her was in control by three different ways:

1. Checking her feelings in the here-and-now. This would include her voice, the words she used, her posture, and the way she sat or walked, as well as how she felt emotionally.
2. Watching how she got along with people. If people around her were upset by bossy Parent messages, they would avoid her or set up conflict situations. If she behaved as Adult, most people around her would be Adult towards her. If the Child in her found expression in happy social situations, other people would enjoy being around her.
3. Looking at feelings about her childhood. By recalling how she talked when she was little and how her mother and father had treated her, Joanne could better understand her present behavior. When she heard herself say things exactly the way her mother or father did, she could be sure she was speaking as Parent.

By the fifth counseling session, Joanne was gaining insight into some of the manipulative games she played with others. She and her therapist had developed a mutual trust and could communicate well in the encounter of therapy. They had begun a tentative exploration of her physical complaints to see if they could find any psychological motivation. In the middle of the session, Joanne said that she wanted to go back to the there-and-then of a few nights ago to describe an important dream to her therapist. After mutually checking with each other to be sure that she wasn't playing a game to keep from working in the here-and-now encounter of the session, they decided to let her talk about her dream. Joanne began:

*I dreamed I was an old black telephone hanging on the wall.
I was in the philosophy room of an old, gothic-type library. I
was covered with dust, and my bell no longer could ring.*

*My mind was rich in the memory of a long time ago when
there were young philosophers in the room with me. They used
me in their research . . . and to make dates with their girlfriends.
I was very important to them then. It didn't matter that I was
plain and black; I was so sturdy and dependable.*

*But then I realized that I'd been replaced by new phones.
Some were red, or yellow, or blue, even a princess model with
push-buttons and video. But I remained the same. I wouldn't let
them transistorize me, so they left me in the old library. I felt
useless, neglected, and very lonely . . . I wished somebody would
call me. I longed to feel useful and needed again. . . .*

Joanne sat quietly after she had finished. Her body language and
facial expression spoke her need to be wanted by someone. Her therapist explained that they could analyze her dream in two ways: the
emotional content in it or what she was feeling after she had shared her
dream with him. Joanne chose to spend the rest of the session talking
about how she was feeling about their relationship. She told her counselor that she felt that perhaps she was making limited progress in
therapy, but that it was difficult for her. She said, "It's easier to talk
about my dreams and fantasies—even how I feel in here with you—than
it is to talk about my life at the house. That scares me."

Joanne started the eighth session by asking her therapist if he had
done further analysis of her "telephone" dream. She wasn't satisfied by
his answer: "A dream has meaning only in terms of the dreamer's symbols. I didn't think it was important unless you said that it was." Joanne
appeared to be unusually nervous. She said she had experienced the
same dream last night and wanted to know if it was an indication that she
was "crazy." Her therapist responded, "Crazy?" Joanne attacked:

*Yes, crazy. That's what I said. Or would you prefer psy-
chotic? There's something ugly and vicious about that word
though. I like just plain crazy. It's more direct and sort of
homey . . . my parents would approve.*

Her therapist countered:

*Joanne, I'm feeling like you set a trap for me. Some kind of
game. You introduced the word crazy and then challenged me to*

*use it or defend it. I sense you're not being quite open with me,
like there is an ulterior transaction going on. . . .*

    *Your voice tone tells me you're angry and anxious, but I
don't know if it is with me, or yourself.*

Joanne accepted his challenge to give up her psychological game.
She said that she honestly did want to talk about some feelings related
to her teaching career.

    *I'd like to go back to when I started teaching and explore
some things. Then we can come back to the here-and-now you
like so much and see what happens. . . .*

    *When I started teaching, even then there were some doubts
in my mind. I guess it was that not OK feeling, but anyway, even
then I had the feeling that something was missing in my life. I
knew it was less than what I really wanted, but I thought . . .
maybe it was one of those things you had to settle for, you
know . . . like a compromise that most of us have to make in the
adult world. . . .*

    *I really wound up living my life according to my parents'
expectations, or at least what I thought they wanted from me.
But last night I was thinking about how empty my life has been,
even before the accident. It just hasn't been enough.*

The therapist asked, "In other words, you're getting selfish?"
Joanne answered:

    *Yes, I guess I am. It's not much of a life. But I'm beginning
to understand it. At least I don't feel guilty as much. I can sense
myself wanting to be more than I am now . . . and maybe be able
to share the best of me with somebody else. . . .*

Joanne's words were followed by her first genuine smile in three weeks
of intensive therapy.

OUTCOME

Part of our cultural heritage is the old schoolbook, *McGuffey's Reader*,
and its passage: "In Adam's fall, we sinned all." Many people in our
society feel that a person is good or bad because there is goodness or

109

badness in them. Parents have accepted the idea that some children are good and others bad; that somehow behavioral patterns and personality characteristics acquired in childhood cannot be changed when the person becomes an adult. This is not true. As human beings we are victims of the reality of the environment that we live in, but we create the reality we understand as our personal lives. Each of us chooses to be rational or irrational, good or bad, happy or sad. We all laugh and cry, but for different reasons.

Joanne has been in therapy for three months now and will probably continue for several months more. Her therapist reports that his TA therapy methods have helped her to see that she is responsible for what happens in her future, no matter what has happened in her past. She has begun to place less confidence in parental dictates and more in her own experience as it occurs within herself. She is less guided by "You should" and "You ought to" feelings. She takes Parent messages into account, as data, but she is no longer ruled by them. In a very real sense, Joanne is beginning to accept the responsibility to choose her own way.

FOCUS QUESTIONS

1. The form of treatment to which a client will respond best depends primarily on how he views the source of his problems. This also depends on his sociological background, verbal skills, and psychological sophistication. How would you approach the mechanics of teaching the "therapy game" to Joanne from the behavioral or client-centered approach?
2. A neurotically depressed person often has a history of poor personal adjustment and may break down emotionally under the strain of daily living. How would you approach a friend or co-worker to convince him he needed "help?" What criteria would you use to decide whether or not you were qualified to provide that help?
3. Some people describe the process of individual therapy in a negative way, using the analogy of a blind man in a dark room looking for a black cat that isn't there. Do you feel that you could objectively "prove" that TA therapy is helping Joanne? How?
4. Oftentimes we greatly underestimate how much of our life is built around our bad habits and the joy they give us. It seems that we don't really want to give them up; we want only to rid ourselves of

the psychological pain they cost us. The alcoholic who gives up drinking is suddenly faced with an empty, lonely life. Most of the psychological games he played with others centered on his drinking habits. Can you identify a personal habit you have that is bad, but not so bad that you will change your behavior?

5. Respect, understanding, and sympathy are proper characteristics for anyone working with children. A black child usually requires more of them than a white child. A black youth is often difficult for a white, middle-class teacher to identify with. What constructive suggestions would you give to a white teacher in a predominantly black high school?

6. The therapist in this case made use of TA counseling techniques. Could you develop a strategy for working with Joanne using client-centered or behavior modification techniques? Outline immediate, intermediate, and outcome goals that you would establish for your counseling approach.

7. What TA games do you play? Can you describe your basic life position? Would you seriously like to change it?

8. Did the fact that Joanne's therapist was old enough to be her father strongly influence this case? Would she have been comfortable with a female therapist? A young male therapist? Would you have been very comfortable working with her?

BIBLIOGRAPHY: JOANNE

Berne, Eric. *Games People Play.* New York: Grove Press, 1964.

_____. *Principles of Group Treatment.* New York: Oxford University Press, 1964.

_____. "Transactional Analysis." In Greenwald, Harold, ed. *Active Psychotherapy.* New York: Atherton Press, 1967.

Harris, Thomas A. *I'm OK—You're OK.* New York: Harper and Row, 1969.

James, M., and Jongeward, D. *Born to Win.* Reading, Mass.: Addison-Wesley, 1971.

McCormick, P., and Campos, L. *Introduce Yourself To Transactional Analysis: A TA Handbook.* Stockton, Calif.: San Joaquin TA Study Group, 1969.

Penfield, W. "Memory Mechanisms." American Medical Association, *Archives of Neurology and Psychiatry* 67 (1952), pp. 178–198.

CRITIQUE OF THE CASE OF JOANNE

Transactional Analysis was the primary therapeutic procedure employed in the case of Joanne; however, the emphasis on the here-and-now, life style, self-responsibility, and dream reporting and analysis also suggest incorporation of Gestalt, Adlerian therapy, reality therapy, and psychoanalytic psychotherapy, respectively. Certainly, it is quite appropriate to utilize what one can from all theoretical positions to assist the client.

Joanne's therapist chose to emphasize TA with her. His description of why he prefers TA, i.e., its special vocabulary that helps to "hook most of my clients into working on their problems," may be a potential liability as well as a potential asset. There are some inherent dangers in giving people a psychological vocabulary to use in labeling. Many people with only a limited understanding of TA have turned it into another game. They are quick to label behavior (usually behavior of others) as Parent, Adult, or Child, but that is as far as it goes. They still don't know how to change it. They often use it more to punish than to help. In other words, developing a therapy vocabulary without knowing how to change inappropriate behavior may do as much to obstruct or impede behavioral change as facilitate it.

But, back to the case of Joanne. Since Joanne was somatotizing her psychological, emotional, and interpersonal deficits, Gestalt therapy (Simkins, in press) would also, at least on the surface, appear to have been a preferred mode of treatment. This hypothesis is strengthened by the apparent need for Joanne to complete unfinished business with her deceased parents, especially since they were taken suddenly out of her life in the automobile accident.

The frequent reporting of dreams by Joanne and her desire to understand them would suggest that she would be a good candidate for psychoanalytic psychotherapy. This position is also substantiated by her conversion hysteria in the forms of debilitating headaches, cramps, and back pains, along with her unresolved relationship with her parents, especially her father. Joanne's lack of meaning in her life also suggests that an existential model would be relevant.

One could continue citing reasons why Joanne's case could have lent itself to any number of possible therapy approaches, but the very fact that each tends to focus on only one or two conditions or client deficits makes most positions incomplete. Since Lazarus (1974a, 1974b) has developed a multimodal therapy that incorporates the best from all the basic therapy models, his model would permit Joanne's problems to be treated most thoroughly. Lazarus views the client from the vantage point of all his sensations plus his interpersonal relationships and his medical state. He focuses on deficits in behavior, affect, sensation, imagery, and cognition in addition to interpersonal relations and medical state. The multimodal model provides the therapist with a relatively complete picture of the client's deficits which allows intervention in *all* the deficit areas rather than focusing primarily on one, e.g., somatic complaints, depression, inadequate interpersonal behavior. Using this model, the therapist could have employed strategies pertinent to each area of deficit and unique to a given therapy model.

There would be two things still deficient in the multimodal approach. First, because it is multimodal, a coherent system of problem-solving (with unique vocabulary, etc.) would be difficult to teach to the client. Secondly, Lazarus' model does not at the moment focus enough on client assets. If assets were included with client deficits (Gazda, Walters, and Childers, in press), the therapist could maximize the intervention strategies. The first deficit can be overcome by teaching the Carkhuff (1969) model, an eclectic therapy model with an inclusive language and comprehensive rationale. The second deficit is handled by determining and recording the client's assets to be utilized throughout treatment.

A few comments on the therapist's actual treatment procedures seem to be in order. First, TA would be an appropriate intervention or therapy mode in the case of Joanne. There seems to be no particular reason, however, why it should be the preferred mode. Since only a few therapist-client interactions were given, only a limited critique is possible. In the second therapy session the therapist "laid some heavy stuff" on the client with an interpretation of her reasons for somatotizing her problems. Her reaction to the confrontation/interpretation indicated that it was probably premature, that the therapist had not invested enough time and effort in building the relationship/base needed before confrontation could be utilized by the client.

Secondly, in the third therapy session the therapist intervened to ask what the client was feeling inside (Parent, Adult, or Child) during her reporting of the dream. An alert therapist would likely have had a good idea how the client felt and would not have to ask. Every time the therapist has to ask a client a question like: "How are you feeling?" the therapist becomes the helpee. Asking the client how he feels also leads to laziness on the part of the therapist.

ADULTS

The therapist's basic tool appeared to be developing client insight with the hope that the client could then change to something better. There was practically no evidence given that the therapist was in fact teaching the client how to change from Parent to Adult behaviors.

During the eighth session the therapist's response to the client's fear that she was "crazy" seemed quite inappropriate. He simply acted as if he didn't understand. "Crazy?" Obviously, she became angry at an apparent gross misunderstanding. Although the therapy following this incident appeared to progress effectively, one wonders if there was any relationship between the two parts of the therapy session.

The therapist concluded the continuing case of Joanne with some evidence that Joanne was making progress. There is, of course, no way of knowing whether this was because of TA or the therapist or which was most influential in her change. Since TA was a meaningful model for the therapist, he could be secure and effective in its use.

Discussion Questions

1. Tell how a reality therapist would have treated the client's talk regarding her physical complaints and her reporting of dreams.
2. What technique might a rational-emotive therapist use in treating the client's repeated use of "no rest for the wicked"?
3. Simulate through role-playing an existential therapy approach to Joanne during an initial interview.
4. Using Lazarus' multimodal model, suggest an intervention strategy for each of the following areas of Joanne's deficits: behavior, affect, sensation, imagery, cognition, interpersonal, medical/drugs. Base your strategies on strengths that (wherever they are indicated in the case report) Joanne possesses.
5. Simulate a session with Joanne in which you use the Gestalt method of "completing unfinished business."

Bibliography: Critique of Joanne

Carkhuff, Robert R. *Helping and Human Relations: A Primer for Lay and Professional Helpers.* Vols. 1 and 2. New York: Holt, Rinehart and Winston, 1969.
Gazda, George M., Walters, Richard P., and Childers, William C. *Human*

Relations Development: A Manual for Health Sciences. Boston: Allyn and Bacon (in press).

Lazarus, Arnold A. "Multimodal Therapy: Basic Id." *Psychology Today* 7, no. 10 (1974), pp 59–63. a.

——— "Multimodal Behavior Therapy in Groups." In Gazda, G. M., ed. *Basic Approaches to Group Psychotherapy and Group Counseling.* Second Edition. Springfield, Ill.: Charles C Thomas, 1974. b.

Simkins, James S. "Gestalt Therapy in Groups." In Gazda, George M. ed. *Basic Approaches to Group Psychotherapy and Group Counseling.* Second Edition. Springfield, Ill.: Charles C Thomas, 1974.

Dee

A college campus is many things to many people; to some it is a place to learn, to others it is a "fun place" to socialize and perhaps to find a husband or wife. For Dee, the college campus is a place to retreat. She uses the classroom as a refuge from the misunderstanding and confusion in her personal life.

Dee is a graduate student completing her coursework for a master's degree in guidance and counseling at a large southern university. She and her husband have been divorced for three weeks. Dee is an intelligent and physically attractive twenty-six-year-old woman. She usually appears to be sure of herself and projects an image of one who is well organized and in command of her thoughts. If two adjectives were used to describe Dee, the most accurate would be: pretty and composed.

As Dee sat in her graduate advisor's office she was not very pretty or composed. Tears streaked her mascara as she struggled to find words to express her confusion and fear. She said:

> *I'm sorry, but I had to talk. . . . I have nobody else to turn to . . . and I feel so miserable, so completely defeated and alone. Everything is going wrong for me, my marriage, even my friends are turning against me. Everything I've worked so hard for is blowing up in my face. I'm afraid I can't take it any more. . . .*

BACKGROUND

Dee grew up in a rural community with her two younger sisters and two younger brothers. She was the first child born to her mother after she

117

had divorced her husband of three years and remarried one year later. Dee described her childhood as happy and carefree and spoke with affection about the unusual closeness in her family. She explained that her parents had the ability to make each of the children feel as though he or she was the most important person in the world. Dee and her family attended the local Baptist church and shared many growing up experiences.

Dee was always an excellent student in school and participated in many extracurricular activities. She was a cheerleader for three years in high school and was elected prom queen in her senior year. Dee had decided that she wanted to become a high school teacher when she was a sophomore. Her vocational decision was strongly influenced by an attractive female English teacher who used her creative talents to inspire and challenge her students to learn about themselves.

Dee described her undergraduate college experience as a very pleasant time in her life. She continued to excel in the classroom and expanded her awareness of the world around her. She dated frequently and enjoyed a variety of social experiences. In her sophomore year, Dee pledged a sorority and lived in the sorority house. She enjoyed her interaction with her sorority sisters and was elected pledge trainer during her junior year. Dee mentioned that she experienced little vocational indecision as she progressed through college. For three summers she was employed as a youth camp counselor and gained valuable experience working with young people. She said:

> It was as if I had always wanted to be a teacher. My summer camp experiences helped to convince me. I was really looking forward to a career in teaching. A lot of my sorority sisters couldn't make up their minds about what they wanted to do. They were really upset. They often came to me to talk about it. Some of them never worked it out and got married instead. But I knew I wanted to be a teacher.

When Dee was a senior in college she chose to live off campus and shared an apartment with two girl friends.

Dee completed her student teaching assignment at a large urban high school located near the university. She was asked to teach three sophomore science classes and a new elective psychology course for seniors. She said that she enjoyed the hectic pace of student teaching and looked forward to the time when she would be working with *her* students. Dee's supervisory teacher was impressed with her enthusiasm, rapport with the students, and organizational ability.

Dee met Stuart on a blind date arranged by one of her roommates. During her senior year they dated frequently and learned to know each other. Dee's graduation was followed by her marriage to Stuart. She explained:

> Stu was a new experience for me. I couldn't believe him. . . . He was unlike anyone else. He was good looking, arrogant . . . but intelligent. None of the other guys I dated were like him. He was just different. . . . He had a way of putting you down, but in a way that made you want to come back for more.
>
> Stuart was easy to talk to and good at sharing ideas. He always had that "special knack" of knowing my mood . . . what would please me. He drank a lot but I passed it off as his need to have a good time with the guys.
>
> I guess what we shared the most was my idealism and his ability to get things done. He was a business administration major—very competitive. Our arguments were usually about his moody periods. He used to get awfully depressed, really down. He would just shut me out for days at a time. Just no contact. Then out of the blue he would be his arrogant, happy self again. I nicknamed him the "Reluctant Dragon." We laughed about it then. . . .

Stuart was an only child and grew up in an unhappy home; his parents had worked out a stormy divorce when he was ten years old. He lived with his mother in a small two-bedroom apartment in metropolitan Kansas City. Stuart told Dee of his early years and of the grim physical battles that took place between his parents. Though both of his parents were religious persons and attended church regularly, they both also drank heavily. They often blamed Stuart for their guilt and disharmony. Beatings had been commonplace events and were unusually severe, administered by his father with an inexorable righteousness. Stuart said that he usually left the apartment when his parents began drinking and returned home only when he thought they had calmed down. He said that he had learned to keep his feelings to himself so that his parents couldn't use them against him. He told Dee that he had not wept since childhood.

Before Dee and Stuart were married, they decided that he should continue his education to receive a master's degree in business administration. Dee agreed to teach freshman biology in a small rural school to support both of them while he worked on his degree. They moved into an apartment complex near the university to take advantage of the cultural activities there. Dee commuted forty miles to teach each morning. They planned to start their family after Stuart graduated and had several years of work experience.

INITIAL COUNSELING INTERVIEW

Dee's graduate advisor recognized her need to talk about her feelings of self-doubt and confusion created by her recent divorce. He thoughtfully closed the door to his office and gave her a few moments to gain her usual composure. He began:

> Dee, I'm willing to work with you in a counseling relationship if that's what you want. . . . You're a good person and I would like to help you if I can. You seem to be confused by some difficult problems that came up all at once. Is that it? Is that what you're feeling?

Dee responded to his counseling invitation by saying:

> Yes, that's how I'm feeling. . . . But I've always thought of counseling as something I'd be doing for someone else. You know, not for me. Until now I always felt OK. Maybe you're right. I know myself on the outside pretty well, but I don't understand myself inside. My divorce shows that. . . . Yeah, I need somebody to help me right now.

Dee and her advisor-counselor worked out an agreement to have two hour-long counseling sessions per week. He told Dee that he would offer his counseling services to her on a no-fee basis as part of his personal commitment to the mental health profession. Dee was not enrolled in any coursework taught by her advisor but had completed his introductory guidance course with a grade of A.

Dee began the first counseling session with a discussion of her first year of marriage. She said that it was a period of groping adjustment and hectic activity for her. She described her relationship with Stuart:

> We really didn't get to know each other that year. We adjusted sexually and all that, but he never gave me the feeling that I could get close to him. He was never around to share ideas . . . that was very important to me. It seemed like he was

120

always gone from the apartment, studying at the library or in class. He went out with the guys pretty often but I didn't complain. I usually didn't have enough energy to want to go. It was easier to stay by myself, I guess. . . .

We joked about me being a commuter casualty. I was so tired all the time. You wouldn't believe how tired I felt. The kids I taught that year were really great. I enjoyed them. I learned a lot about myself as a teacher that first year. The other teachers accepted my mistakes and helped me out.

It was during the summer after her first year of teaching that Dee began to notice serious cracks in the foundation of her marriage. She was free from teaching obligations and looked forward to spending more time with Stuart. She hoped to deepen the caring relationship they had formed during courtship. It didn't happen. Dee said that instead of drawing closer together in their marriage, they began to grow further apart. Stuart spent less and less time with her at the apartment.

Dee traced the development of her feeling of "something wrong" to a significant incident that occurred shortly after she finished teaching in the spring. Stuart had applied for a teaching assistantship in the business department. He wanted it very much for financial and prestige reasons. He thought he was sure to get it, but at the last moment it was awarded to someone else. Stuart reacted by developing a bitter resentment toward his graduate training and claimed that the department was loaded with old phonies hiding from the real business world. Instead of sharing his disappointment with Dee, Stuart disappeared for two days. When he returned to the apartment he pointed with arrogant amusement at the new expensive sportscar he had purchased. He called it his mood elevator and became irrational when Dee asked him to explain his absence. He informed Dee that he had taken a job tending bar in a local pub to make the payments on the car.

I was furious . . . and so was he. He just wouldn't listen to me. Nothing I said could get through to him. I felt cut off . . . shut out. . . . So I took the old car and went home to visit my family. I didn't know what else to do. I sensed that we had stopped reaching out for each other. That was the first time he ever totally shut me out.

In the fall of her second year of marriage, Dee entered graduate school on a part-time basis. She and Stuart had developed serious marital problems related to what she called his silent treatment and extended absences from the apartment. She chose to seek graduate training in guidance and counseling because "it sounded interesting. I was afraid to be alone in the apartment so much. I thought that learning about how to help other people might help me solve some of our problems."

Dee enjoyed the adult comradeship of her two graduate courses and did very well. She often made practical application of the guidance principles she was learning to her classroom teaching. Dee had an unusual ability to communicate warmth and acceptance toward those around her. She found it easy to share her enthusiasm for helping others find workable solutions to their problems.

It was ironic that, as Dee was making excellent progress toward her goal of becoming a counselor, her marriage to Stuart was failing. Dee explained:

> I felt like a Jekyll-Hyde. At night I was learning to be a counselor and during the day my marriage was falling apart. It started getting pretty bad last fall. Stuart was treating me more like a roommate and less like his wife.
>
> We . . . uhhh . . . we started having sex problems about then, too. You see, he never seemed interested in me. Not that way, anyway. He was gone from the apartment all the time. When he came home he would just crawl in behind the paper. No talk, no explanation, no nothing. . . .

In the middle of the fall semester, Stuart decided to withdraw completely from his graduate program. He told Dee that he couldn't concentrate on his studies anymore, and he felt that the professors were prejudiced against him. He said that he didn't want to finish a meaningless program. After telling Dee about his decision, Stuart disappeared from their apartment. Dee was forced to interrupt his absence two days later when she learned of his mother's death through a phone call from a neighbor. When Dee went to the pub where Stuart worked, she received equally bad news; Stuart was living in an apartment with a waitress who worked at the pub.

Dee told her counselor:

> That did it. Any relationship we had created up to that point—my trust and respect—was suddenly washed away. It cut me deeply and I didn't know what to think. I had no idea . . . no suspicion. . . . Wow! How could I have been so stupid!

When Stuart came back from his mother's funeral, he offered Dee little explanation about his affair. He agreed to stop seeing the girl and apologized for not telling Dee. He said that he couldn't understand why he began the affair. When Dee suggested that they see a marriage counselor, Stuart suddenly became angry and said:

> *Stop trying to therapize me! I don't need you. You just want too much, that's all. There's nothing wrong with me. You want to own me—possess me—know everything about me—but I don't want you to. Can't you see that? Leave me alone. I'm sick of living my life like I was in a straight-jacket.*

When Dee finished talking about Stuart's refusal to participate in marital counseling, she was visibly shaken. She turned her face toward her counselor and looked as if she were asking him to hear something she could not say. Dee's brittle emotional edge had shown through her smooth social manners. In a few moments she became poised and controlled enough to say, "Well, let's go on."

The next crisis in Dee's marriage happened several weeks later. Dee said that her relationship with Stuart had become almost nonexistent. He was working full-time at the pub to keep up the car payments and was seldom home when Dee was there. Dee explained:

> *He became sort of a silent partner. Yeah, that's it. A silent partner. We didn't communicate at all. He just sat around. We didn't talk. We didn't make love, nothing. I got the feeling he resented my presence in the apartment, didn't want me around.*

> *Stuart stopped being sexy for me. He almost never came near me, and when he did, it was over so fast. Like he was in a hurry to get it over with . . . to get rid of me or get away from me. That's how he made me feel. He would just come in the door and crawl in behind that damn paper. He wasn't interested in me anymore.*

Soon Dee began to suspect that if Stuart wasn't interested in her, he might be interested in someone else. She was right. Stuart had begun another affair with a girl he met at the pub. Dee found out about it when a girl friend mentioned that she had seen Stuart playing tennis with a pretty, blonde girl. When Dee confronted Stuart with her information, he admitted that he was interested in the girl. He denied sexual involvement with her but insisted that nothing was wrong with an occasional extramarital "date" if both partners agreed. Dee pointed out that she had *not* agreed and never would agree to Stuart's "dating" other women as long as she was married to him. "In fact," she said, "if you want your freedom, why don't you just pack your things and leave now." Stuart accepted her heated challenge; he packed his things and left the apartment.

When Dee learned later that Stuart was living with his girlfriend, she initiated divorce proceedings. She told her counselor:

> *I think that's when I hit rock-bottom emotionally. I was really low, you know. I decided to quit trying to save our marriage. I knew it wouldn't be easy to admit failure, but I had to start somewhere. My feelings were all twisted . . . I thought maybe I still loved him . . . but I hated him for the way he had treated me. . . .*

Dee's counselor began to form the ending of the first counseling session when he encouraged her to try to describe what she felt was her most important counseling goal. Dee answered:

> *Well, I guess I want to find out who I am—understand myself. I feel guilty . . . but I want a chance to prove that I am a good person, in spite of my broken marriage. I've really been depressed and anxious . . . I know it takes two people to have problems and I can't figure out what I did wrong. I just wish he was here to give his side of it . . . to tell you what was wrong with me. . . .*

Although Dee's counselor felt that he understood what she was trying to say, he reminded her, "It would be nice if Stuart was here to answer and willing to cooperate, but he isn't. You'll have to work it through alone, with me."

The counselor responded to Dee's need to know herself better by asking her to take the Taylor-Johnson Temperament Analysis Profile (T-JTA). He explained that it was a test designed to provide an evaluation in visual form, showing a person's feelings about herself at the time she answered the questions. An advantage of the test was that Dee could have someone else who knew her well answer the test questions in an effort to provide more information about Dee's personality. Dee agreed and said that she would ask a friend who had taught with her to fill the test out. The first counseling session ended when the counselor said:

Dee, next time we should talk more about you and your feelings. You talked a lot about Stuart, and he wasn't even here. It could be that it was easier for you to talk about him, rather than yourself. We need to explore your feelings about you . . . and maybe outline what you think your important problems are.

COUNSELING METHODOLOGY

Psychobehavioral counseling and therapy does not qualify as a new theory because it does not offer a unique explanation of personality development. It does, however, offer an important frame of reference for the counselor who would like to integrate effective behavioral therapy methods into insight-oriented counseling. Psychobehavioral counseling makes use of the implicit assumption that insight and behavioral approaches have the potential for a reciprocally beneficial integration.

R. H. Woody, in his book, *Psychobehavioral Counseling and Therapy*, described the significant advantages of this approach:

It allows the counselor-therapist to accept either the psycho-dynamic viewpoint of the insightists or the conditioning viewpoint of the actionists or behaviorists, thereby offering no boundaries to personality theory or other aspects requisite for a full-blown theory of counseling or therapy. Therefore, psychobehavioral counseling and therapy denotes a technical eclecticism, with special emphasis on the use of both insight and conditioning techniques and the role of the counselor-therapist as the person significantly responsible for the counseling-therapeutic action.

The key importance of the psychobehavioral approach to counseling is the blending, with theoretical justification and professional skill, of what might seem to be contradictory counseling techniques. The psychologist is offered an opportunity to maintain a theoretical position based on his choice of a comprehensive counseling theory and to augment it with behavior modification techniques.

The basic counseling orientation of Dee's counselor was client-centered. He believed that most individuals have a natural drive to become worthwhile, unique persons. He tried to understand the internal frame of reference of the people he counseled with by thinking, feeling, and exploring things related to their personal problems. He felt that the most important role of the counselor was to provide a warm, nonthreatening atmosphere in which his client could explore his true feelings openly and honestly. He encouraged his clients to lower their defenses and explore their own capabilities as they reached out for a sense of meaning. During his counseling sessions he consciously said things designed to reflect and clarify the emotional state of his client.

Dee's counselor chose to supplement his client-centered counseling approach with two important behavior modification techniques— problem identification and goal evaluation. The problem identification process was based on the assumption that goals for counseling have to be clarified before the means for obtaining them can be determined. The counselor's years of experience told him that he could facilitate the emotional growth of his clients more quickly if they understood where they wanted to go.

In the early counseling sessions the counselor worked with his client to develop a caring relationship and to identify what the basic problem was. He encouraged his client to accept the responsibility for determining his own counseling goals. By creating client awareness of specific counseling objectives, the counselor could then help his client monitor his progress. The goal evaluation process was accomplished by objectively checking the client's behavior to see if the original counseling goals had been accomplished.

It seemed logical to Dee's counselor that, just as an individual must have articulation between what he is doing in life and what he perceives as worthwhile goals, so should the counselor perceive articulation between his counseling processes and outcome goals. For that reason, he divided his counseling methodological approach into three parts: (1) immediate goals, (2) intermediate goals, and (3) outcome goals. Immediate goals in his counseling relationships focused on establishing rapport and communication with his client. His counseling behavior was directed by his need to learn how deeply he could probe with his client for insight and motivation behind his client's problem. This process enabled the counselor to lay the procedural foundation for future counseling sessions.

Intermediate goals in the counseling process were related to the counselor's efforts to help his client learn about alternative choices of behavior. After each verbal action and reaction, the client and counselor have created more structure in their relationship. The topic may be narrowed from female sexual behavior to the client's personal prob-

lem of sexual adjustment in marriage. It is usually during the intermediate portion of the counseling process that the client gains insight
and new understanding of his past behavior. He often reaches out toward new alternatives and begins to behave differently. As the commu-
nicative counseling experience continues to focus more sharply on the
client's anxiety producing situation, the counselor can gradually increase the emphasis of movement toward the counseling outcome goals
chosen by his client.

For Dee's counselor, the ultimate goal of counseling and therapy
was self-competency for his client. He purposely substituted the term
self-competency for more popular terms like fully functioning or self-
actualizing. To him, self-competency meant just that. The counselor was responsible for helping his client to become competent or
aware enough to make sound and rational judgments about his own
behavior.

Prior to the second counseling session with Dee, her counselor reviewed his therapeutic notes from the first session. He recalled that she
was having difficulty in two areas: (1) anxiety about her recent divorce
from Stuart and (2) emotional confusion about her own self-worth. The
Taylor-Johnson test that Dee and her friend had completed offered him
some interesting information.

Individuals who score in the area which is shaded darkest have the
best adjustment in interpersonal relationships, while those scoring in
the white area may have serious problems. Dee's profile (solid lines)
indicated that she felt her personality characteristics were usually more
than adequate. The single trait score that was in the white area was
submissiveness, an indication of self-doubt and feelings of insecurity. In
a marital relationship, a high degree of submissiveness implies a willingness to follow rather than lead. The profile created for Dee by her
friend (dotted lines) supported Dee's scores.

The second counseling interview began when the counselor asked
Dee, "How are you feeling today?" Dee answered:

> *Confused. I'm still looking for answers . . . something to hold
> on to. I feel better than when I saw you the first time, but I'm
> still mixed up. I know I'm angry about what Stuart did to me; it
> will take time to work that one out.*

> *I've been thinking about him a lot, you know, and about
> what you said last time. It's not easy to sort out my thoughts
> and decide what you want from counseling. I know I want to*

ADULTS

TAYLOR-JOHNSON TEMPERAMENT ANALYSIS PROFILE
Profile Revision of 1967

These Answers Describe **Ms Dee ——** Age **26** Sex **F** Date **——**

School **State Univ.** Grade ____ Degree **Med** Major **Guidance** Occupation **Teacher** Counselor **J.M.**

Single **X** Years Married **2** Years Divorced **O** Years Widowed ____ Children: M ____ Ages ____ F ____ Ages ____

Answers made by: SELF **and** husband, wife, father, mother, son, daughter, brother, sister, or **Teacher - Friend** of the person described.

Norm(s):	A	B	C	D	E	F	G	H	I	Attitude (Sten) Score: **6 5**
Mids	**2**		**1 1**		**2**	**1**		**3**	**2 1 1**	Total Mids: **9 5**
Raw score	**12 10**	**8**	**6**	**31 33**	**36 38**	**38 38**	**7 6**	**10 17**	**12 5**	**33 28**	Raw score
Percentile	**51 36**	**42**	**32**	**72 81**	**80 95**	**87 94**	**32 24**	**9 27**	**12 22**	**83 64**	Percentile
TRAIT	Nervous	Depressive	Active-Social	Expressive-Responsive	Sympathetic	Subjective	Dominant	Hostile	Self-disciplined	TRAIT

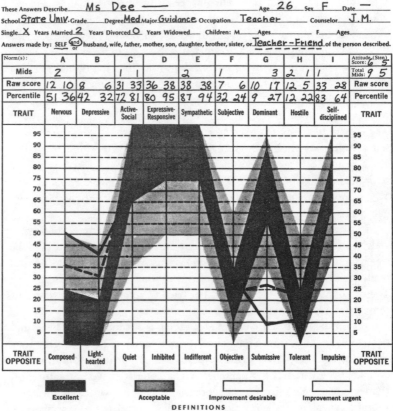

| TRAIT OPPOSITE | Composed | Light-hearted | Quiet | Inhibited | Indifferent | Objective | Submissive | Tolerant | Impulsive | TRAIT OPPOSITE |

Excellent   Acceptable   Improvement desirable   Improvement urgent

DEFINITIONS

TRAITS

Nervous — Tense, high-strung, apprehensive.
Depressive — Pessimistic, discouraged, dejected.
Active-Social — Energetic, enthusiastic, socially involved.
Expressive-Responsive — Spontaneous, affectionate, demonstrative.
Sympathetic — Kind, understanding, compassionate.
Subjective — Emotional, illogical, self-absorbed.
Dominant — Confident, assertive, competitive.
Hostile — Critical, argumentative, punitive.
Self-disciplined — Controlled, methodical, persevering.

OPPOSITES

Composed — Calm, relaxed, tranquil.
Light-hearted — Happy, cheerful, optimistic.
Quiet — Socially inactive, lethargic, withdrawn.
Inhibited — Restrained, unresponsive, repressed.
Indifferent — Unsympathetic, insensitive, unfeeling.
Objective — Fair-minded, reasonable, logical.
Submissive — Passive, compliant, dependent.
Tolerant — Accepting, patient, humane.
Impulsive — Uncontrolled, disorganized, changeable.

Note: Important decisions should not be made on the basis of this profile without confirmation of these results by other means.

Taylor-Johnson Temperament Analysis *(T-JTA), Taylor, Robert M., and Morrison, Lucile Phillips, Psychological Publications, Inc., 5300 Hollywood Blvd., Los Angeles, Calif., 90027, 1966–1973. Reproduced by permission.*

feel better about myself and where I'm going, but that's too general.

Did the test tell you anything more specific?

Dee and her counselor looked at her scores on the T-JTA profile and talked about her trait score in the area of submissiveness. Dee said that she didn't think the score was representative of her normal behavior. She pointed out that while she was more submissive than usual in her marital role with Stuart, she didn't consider herself to be very submissive in other personal relationships.

Dee's explanation of her unusually submissive role in her relationship with Stuart led to a discussion of how she developed her self-image as a divorcee. Dee seemed to have three mental pictures of herself. One image was herself as she thought others expected her to be. It was a romanticized blending of all of her good and pleasant traits, coupled with her physical beauty. Each positive aspect of her personality was overstated and extreme. Dee hoped that she would someday become that person.

The second self-image Dee described was a scaled-down, more human version of the first image. It was more realistic. Her imperfections were apparent, but they were ordinary shortcomings that many people shared. This image included problems related to past mistakes and poor judgment.

It was the third image that disturbed Dee. It was a picture of a barely recognizable self; her faults were presented in a totally negative way. She saw herself as an inconsiderate, selfish person who was unworthy of anyone's attention. She felt she was unable to perform satisfactorily as a sexual partner and wife.

Dee's problems seemed to stem from her feelings about her third self-image. She thought it was her real self. She told her counselor:

> *It's like I have three different identities. One is what I project to people I want to like me. That one is set up by what the situation demands. The second image is the person that comes out when I'm with my friends. It goes along with what I look like and how people accept me. You know, some good and some bad. The third person . . . she's a total failure. When I'm alone for a while, I become that third person. I'm thinking that's really me, if you dig down deep enough. . . .*

The counselor recognized that each of Dee's three images was correct in one sense. Each image reflected life's reality filtered through

Dee's past experiences. She was allowing her marital defeat to dominate her total personality. In a stable, well-organized person, there should be a high degree of similarity and continuity from one self-image to the next. Dee's view of herself appeared to be temporarily out of focus.

During the early counseling sessions, Dee and her counselor had developed a mutual caring relationship. The counselor felt it was now time to work toward eliciting Dee's awareness of specific counseling objectives. The third meeting was structured by the counselor to help Dee identify what she considered to be her most difficult problem. He asked Dee:

> Let's see if we can put some kind of structure—a priority—to your problems as you see them. Working from false assumptions will only lead us to faulty solutions. Working toward the real problems might be uncomfortable, but it is the only way you can find long-term solutions.
>
> I want you to write down a list of five things that are really troubling you today. Put them in rank order, from the most important to the least. When you're done, we'll go over your list together.

The purpose of having Dee write her list down on paper was to demonstrate to her that there were objective ways to deal with subjective feelings and problems. The list she created would give her a chance to experience the responsibility for determining her own counseling agenda.

After ten minutes, Dee had listed five things that were troubling her:

1. Feel bad about what I'm doing with my life
2. Want to know what kind of person I *really* am
3. Divorce and accepting my failure
4. Lack of friends who will accept me as I am now
5. Need to teach myself to reach out for new experiences

As Dee and her counselor began to talk about her list, she made the observation that all five of the things she had listed were things that she could control. She and her counselor spent the remainder of the session talking about how she could create experiences that might help her understand the purpose of her life.

Dee began the fifth interview by saying that she was very depressed.

She explained that last night she had gone on her first date. She was close to tears as she told her counselor:

> *It was awful! It just didn't work out like I had it planned at all. I was so nervous before he picked me up, and then all through the meal I kept thinking we would meet someone I knew. What would they think about me. I'm sure he had a terrible time. After it was all over, I just went to bed and cried and cried. . . . This morning I feel so stupid and frustrated. I know I shouldn't, but I still do. I'm really a mess.*

Her counselor responded:

> *Dee, you're not helpless . . . and you know it. I can appreciate the anxiety and frustration you feel this morning, but I'm getting frustrated, too. I think you should stop talking about your failures and feeling bad in general, and start talking about what you can do for yourself, Dee.*
>
> *You and I both know that you are attractive, bright, sophisticated, and have good insight. You've also made it clear that you are choosing to concentrate your thoughts on your negative, self-defeating image. For some reason, you don't want to let go of your bad thoughts about yourself. To be honest with you, I'm getting angry about that.*

What the counselor was doing, essentially, was to interpret Dee's behavior as a defense against working on what was really bothering her. He knew that depression often masks anger. It is the defense mechanism that represents the struggle between two opposing feelings—love and hate. Caught in the struggle to express two honest-but-opposite feelings toward Stuart, Dee had become unable to express either emotion. She was dealing with her anger by turning it inward and then denying its expression. The counselor felt that Dee's depression stemmed from her belief in her own helplessness. His abrupt counseling methods were calculated to take away from her the approach she found most comfortable—repressing her anger and masking it in depression. He wanted her to become frustrated enough with him to bring her anger to the surface and express it.

His plan worked. Dee stared at the wall space just above the counselor's head and bit her lip. For a moment her face was without any expression. Then she exploded:

*All right! I'm getting angry too. All of a sudden you don't
seem to give a damn about me or how I feel today. That's not
right. I need your help, and you tell me you're angry. What am I
supposed to do? Sit here and spill out all my problems for you
to look at and then go home to wait for our next session? That
makes me angry too. Can't you see that?*

The counselor answered Dee's challenge:

*Good. I'm glad you're angry with me. You can't be angry
and depressed at the same time. Dee, I wanted you to get upset
with me for a good reason. I think your depression is a cover-up
for what you feel toward Stuart because he left you. But instead
of swearing at him or attacking him physically, you somehow
turn your anger inward. You bottle it up inside of you and then
feel guilty about hating him. You seem so much prettier when
you fool yourself. It's not pleasant to look in the mirror or to
look at some of the unpleasant things that need to be looked at.
Instead, you've been getting depressed and convinced yourself
that you've become a failure. . . .*

*I wanted to give you a chance to release some of your frus-
tration and see your behavioral cycle in action. At least you
trusted me enough to get mad and express your anger. Do you
understand, Dee?*

Dee agreed that she was no longer depressed. She told the counselor
that his example was clear enough, but she needed time to think over
what he had said about how she became depressed. They closed the
session with an agreement to meet again two days later.

In the next three counseling sessions Dee and her counselor worked
on ways for her to identify and separate feelings of love, hate, anger,
futility, and depression. As Dee struggled to break through the tangle of
habitual self-deception, she began to make significant progress toward
understanding her own life. In the eighth counseling session Dee said:

*You know, I've been trying not to reach back for negative
feelings anymore. I want to leave Stuart behind me now, even
though there are still some rough spots. . . . I understand now
that there were places I couldn't go with him. When he got in a
mood and shut me out, I kept trying to reach him. I never made
it. That's where I hooked myself into thinking I was a failure and
got depressed.*

I think I'm ready to move on now. I'm finding out that I have some private places, too. I'm ready to see the positive side to my life again. I feel like I was drowning in my frustration and depression. You know, going down for the third time. But suddenly I can swim again. I'm looking at all of my qualities now, good and bad, and trying to accept them as a natural part of me. If I can learn to accept myself, the person I want to become will be the person I really am.

At the beginning of the tenth counseling session, Dee told her counselor that she thought it would probably be her last session. An important experience had taken place over the weekend. Dee shared it with her counselor:

I was driving along, coming back from the teacher's workshop. I was pretty tired and getting sleepy, so I decided to stop. I got out and climbed to the top of a big hill that just happened to be there. For a while I thought about how I felt as a divorcee. I decided that I feel used, cheapened somehow. I know I shouldn't feel it . . . my mind says so . . . but it's there and I felt it. It isn't the end of the world to break up a marriage if it doesn't work, but it just seemed like I was left with bits and pieces of my life. Such an empty feeling. . . .

Then, for the first time after three years of marriage, I really felt alone. All alone. Just me and my big hill. I think I found the courage to move beyond my problems up there. Does that sound crazy? I know we've been working on having new experiences, but. . . . Anyway, I think I found me on that hill—and I liked myself. I felt good about me.

The counseling relationship between Dee and her counselor came to an end when he said:

Dee, it seems to me that there are two ways to grow: one is through our interaction with other people who care about us. The other is self-learning through solitude. Sometimes we get to know ourselves only through self-reflection and meditation. When we listen and try to understand what our mind and body are telling us, we can create a better way for our own life. I'm happy that you like yourself.

SUMMARY

In our society, young people commonly marry in a romantic haze. They marry an image, not a real person. The image is partly a construction of their own needs and fantasies and partly a result of deliberate contrivance on the part of the other. The other person presents himself as the kind of person he thinks will be loved and accepted, but seldom offers a true picture of his personality. Regrettably, the marriage of Stuart and Dee seemed to illustrate what happens to young people who lose their first encounter in the marriage game.

Dee's divorce from Stuart presented a major challenge to her self-concept as a worthwhile person. But Dee was fortunate. Her ability to shape words to express her dark thoughts of self-doubt and depression accelerated her emotional recovery. An important factor in Dee's improved psychological adjustment was her ability to recognize the behavioral cycle which caused her depression.

Dee visited her counselor for a total of ten counseling sessions during a period of five weeks. At the start of her counseling experience, Dee desperately needed reassurance and emotional support. She needed to know that she was a worthwhile person, apart from her ex-husband. The counselor made effective use of client-centered counseling methods while he integrated the behavior modification techniques of problem identification and goal evaluation. Two consistent threads ran through each counseling session: one was Dee's desire for personal freedom and the other was her need for acceptance and longing for a relatedness to another person. Dee terminated the counseling process because she felt she had achieved her primary goal—"to find out who I am—understand myself."

FOCUS QUESTIONS

1. There are many emotionally stable individuals in our society who are temporarily overwhelmed by a personal crisis. Dee seemed to be one of them. Could any caring, emphatic person who offered psychological support have helped her?
2. Married young couples of today live in a high-speed technological world that knows only rapid change. New and complex life styles seem to call for a new marriage format. What changes in the marriage relationship could have helped Dee and Stuart?

3. Sexual frustration in marriage often leads to anger and hostility, followed by guilt about being angry. Can you suggest how young couples might work together to prevent such circumstances?

4. A choice that confronts everyone who receives counseling is this: Shall I let my counselor know me as I am now, or should I encourage him to see me as I want to be seen? The counselee often camouflages her true feelings to protect herself against criticism or rejection. How honest do you think Dee was?

5. Dee wasn't enrolled in coursework taught by her advisor-counselor when she sought him out for counseling. Do you think a counselor-educator should extend counseling services to his students?

6. Dee's mother divorced her first husband after three years of marriage. Stuart's parents worked out a stormy divorce when he was ten years old. Do you think these circumstances affected their marriage?

7. Some of the events that may set off reactive depression are familiar to each of us: death of loved ones, physical disease, or financial problems. What these experiences have in common is the sense of one's own helplessness and the futility of life. Can you suggest alternative ways to combat depression?

8. The one-to-one relationship between Dee and her counselor gave her a chance to fulfill her human needs: the developmental and psychological needs for trust, intimacy, and the sharing of experiences. Do you think Dee would have found group counseling as effective as individual therapy was?

9. It takes all kinds and there are all kinds. A voyeur finds it necessary to look rather than to do. As a counselor it would be easy to look at the secrets and problems of others to reassure oneself about his own stability. Do you think Dee would become a good counselor?

BIBLIOGRAPHY: DEE

Woody, Robert H. *Psychobehavioral Counseling and Therapy.* New York: Appleton-Century-Crofts, 1971.

CRITIQUE OF THE CASE OF DEE

The case of Dee raises an ethical question regarding the counseling of an advisee by an advisor. The revised American Personnel and Guidance Association's Ethical Standards allows for this kind of relationship only under unusual circumstances, viz., that the person seeking help has little or no other possibilities available and that the relationship is voluntary. The latter condition seemed to exist in this case, but there is little evidence that the counselor made a serious effort to refer his advisee.

The model for counseling selected for Dee, i.e., psychobehavioral, would seem appropriate provided that it was adequately implemented. As the case is presented there is some reason to doubt that it was. First, there seemed to be very little value in administering the Taylor-Johnson Temperament Analysis Profile when the counselee's problem was so obvious. Secondly, the goal of "self-competency" was so general that it would be difficult to know when it had been achieved. The behavioral aspect of the psychobehavioral model demands more specificity in goal setting than self-competency. The counselor, therefore, should have encouraged the counselee to be more specific in goal setting, as he did in the third session when he asked Dee to list five things that were troubling her.

The counselor's abrupt confrontation, evaluative behavior, and self-disclosure of anger toward the counselee represent a dubious technique. It is this type of unpredictable counselor behavior (technique oriented) that would lead many counselees to lose trust in their counselor. The explanation of Dee's depression was quite likely accurate, but the direct manipulation of her to get her angry with the counselor so that he could teach her this lesson through his deception of being angry seems questionable at best. The counselee would have to wonder in the future if the counselor's feelings were real or whether he was role-playing just to elicit a particular response from her.

The counselor's behavior—his manipulations, confrontations, and interpretations—hardly places him in the client-centered framework that he espoused, at least in his practice of it.

Although the psychobehavioral model would be appropriate to use with Dee, the Carkhuff (1969) model would likely have given the counselor more guidelines and theoretical rationale for his intervention.

Discussion Questions

1. Compare and contrast Carkhuff's counseling model (1969) with the psychobehavioral model of Woody outlined in the case of Dee. Which of these models provides you with the most direction?
2. Describe how Albert Ellis' rational emotive therapy could be applied to the case of Dee.
3. Simulate through role-playing the Gestalt approach to counseling Dee during the first interview.
4. Discuss the ethical issues involved in a teacher counseling his students (subordinates).

Bibliography: Critique of Dee

Carkhuff, Robert R. *Helping and Human Relations: A Primer for Lay Helpers.* Vol. 1. *Selection and Training.* New York: Holt, Rinehart and Winston, 1969.